AMERICAN CULTURE AND THE NIGERIAN SOCIETY

by

Innocent Emechete

Bloomington, IN  Milton Keynes, UK

 authorHOUSE®

AuthorHouse™
1663 Liberty Drive, Suite 200
Bloomington, IN 47403
www.authorhouse.com
Phone: 1-800-839-8640

AuthorHouse™ UK Ltd.
500 Avebury Boulevard
Central Milton Keynes, MK9 2BE
www.authorhouse.co.uk
Phone: 08001974150

First published by AuthorHouse 1/2/2007

ISBN: 978-1-4259-8247-8 (sc)
ISBN: 978-1-4259-8248-5 (hc)

Library of Congress Control Number: 2006910517

Printed in the United States of America
Bloomington, Indiana
This book is printed on acid-free paper.

DEDICATION

This book is dedicated to the Ekechukwu Ukonu and Emechete Anyanwu Anyaku Ojimadu Okwuba Families for the moral heritage they left their children. May God reward them eternally for their moral contribution to our society!

ACKNOWLEDGEMENTS

I wish to use this space to thank God for giving me the courage and energy to write the book, *American Culture And The Nigerian Society*. I also thank all those who in anyway consciously or unconsciously, helped me to write it. A lot of people influenced the writing of this book without even knowing it. There are people, whom I observed on the streets or on television; there are some who took the laws into their own hands against the Constitution of the United States of America; there are others who turned or helped to turn the Constitution upside down; they all formed part of the substance of the book. Without them I would not have even thought of writing this book. To them I say, 'thanks' for providing the material and the incentive. I thank Fr. Jude T. Ezeji, Sister Francisca Nzeke and Sister Patricia Ebegbulem, who all read the original manuscript under a different title, for their encouragement to publish it. Lastly I wish to thank Mr. Bobby D. for providing me with some of the books and court decisions that I read in preparation for the book.

PREFACE

In order to fully understand our use of the term "culture" in this book, *American Culture and the Nigerian society,* it is appropriate that we closely look at the word. Many dictionaries are basically in agreement with the different ways it is used. Culture is the act of developing the intellectual and moral faculties of man. It can be described as the enlightenment and the highest standard of taste acquired by training the mind to acknowledge and appreciate beauty in general and fine art in particular.

Culture is exhibited in beliefs, social forms, racial traits, religion and social groups including the people's attitudes, values, goals and practices and customs shared by a people. In a simple description, culture can be said to be the ways of a people; the way they think, the way they talk, the food they eat, how they pray, or do business or just the way they live their lives.

In *American Culture and the Nigerian Society,* we set out to see how the way Americans think, talk, eat, socialize, believe and pray can affect the Nigerian Society and their cultural traits. Since culture is not static, it grows, it improves or deteriorates; it can borrow from other cultures and be borrowed from. It is transferred from one cultural group to another. What the reader will see is an attempt to look into how the way Americans go to the polls, the way they think, and practice their faith affect an African Country many thousands of miles away on the other side of the Atlantic.

The United States of America and Nigeria were under survey to examine their values by comparing and contrasting them. At different times in history, both Nigeria and America were under the "Union

Jack" of Great Britain. We looked at what brought America and Nigeria together and the circumstances of the marriage of convenience. Like many other relationships and political marriages between countries, there is always a selfish motive to them. In the whole of Africa, Nigeria is one of the strongest allies of the United States in so many ways. Consequently there is an exchange of goods: social, economic and intellectual. Where there is a free flow of ideas and personnel, the good, the bad and the ugly pass through also. In looking into the American people and their culture with all the attendant issues and problems: crime and punishment, drugs, bastardized sexual attitudes, exploitation of God-given freedom and commercialization of religion, we were curious as to how these influences could affect a comparatively young nation in Africa. With our familiarization with the two countries, we were sufficiently equipped to make necessary evaluations of the two cultures and offer some advice to the weaker nation, Nigeria. The first question was to find out if some of these American problems had infiltrated into the Nigerian society during the course of these thirty something years of social and economic relationship. If the answer is affirmative, is this an asset? If not, what could Nigeria do before it is too late?

America, of course, did not wake-up one morning with social problems. The twenties, thirties, forties and even the fifties were morally American Golden Years. In our investigation we found out that things fell apart in the sixties with the "hippie era". That ushered in the sexual revolution, the age of enquiry and liberation. From there on, heaven broke loose. Rebellion was born in every family and every city of the United States. America started to see fashion with some attitude. Parents started to lose parental grip on their children. Mother and daughter removed their "shackles" and went to the city, changed their wardrobe and tried their first cigarette.

The Founding Fathers of America paid their first visit in a very long time and were surprised at what they saw. The Constitution they put together was still there but their interpretation did not look familiar. The insightful inclusion of the Amendments to the Constitution was beginning to look like a curse that continues to unfold into more and more headaches for the Nation. The First Amendment became the lighting rod for National moral disaster, socially and economically.

The Black population, which was struggling for integration into the American society, got sucked into an economic marginalization ever since. The social and moral parameters were degraded. Young people were miss-guided; they lost their youth, social and religious moral sense. The Black communities suffered most because of the background they were coming out from – from slavery, seeking equality and fell into false "freedom" and revolution. Their liberation came at the time the rest of America was being introduced to another kind of freedom, the false freedom. Unfortunately they first freedom they embraced was not real. The shock devastated a whole people and pushed a good number into poverty and crime. That stigma can still be seen lingering around Black American Communities from city to city and from prison to prison. Is there any wonder why more than fifty percent of incarcerated Americans are African American? The Constitution was designed to free the people; but it ended up enslaving people, black and white, in their consciences and in their homes because of miss-application of some of the Amendments.

The dignity of the American women was further degraded when seven of the nine men in the Supreme Court of the United States of America in January of 1973 granted women the permission to kill their babies if they choose to. The value of human life was curtailed. Taking away human life became easy and fashionable. The choice to do evil suddenly became a good thing. Other evil behaviors took their queue from abortion 'choice'. American women were looking to be liberated; but they unfortunately became slaves of their own passions as well as becoming the objects of passion. They in turn enslaved their men. This slavery took the entire Nation hostage. A host of other moral, social as well as economic, destabilizing issues came out of that choice, thanks to Justice Blackmun and six other Justices of the Supreme Court of the United States of America.

The new America set sail with an agenda within and without her borders. The doctrine of "The Separation of Church and State" was born. That created a battle between "Church and State", both of which serve the spiritual and temporal welfare of the same people. Meanwhile unnecessary wounds have been inflicted on both sides and the confused and ordinary people are still suffering from those wounds. Another area of casualty is the Church relinquishing some of her areas of expertise, her moral high ground and bowed to a flat moral relativism to conform to the civil authority. When the Preacher has been converted by the one he was preaching to and the one trying to exorcize the possessed person was, possessed by the same demon he chased out, the church lost a big chunk of her moral authority. And that is a pity and contributes to our societal problems.

On the foreign sector, many nations have been sold the bad seeds growing in the home front. Nigeria is one of the beneficiary nations in question. There is a call to stop the ill wind before it becomes too strong to stop. Fortunately Nigeria has one big advantage which some nations don't have. She has a very strong sense of family and a deep religious foundation. Church dissent will not catch on easily in Nigeria for the same reason. The "alternative life" issue is another American export which will not prosper in the Nigerian society. Hopefully the seed already planted will not gain any ground there. The so-called alternative life style is, however, a disgusting concept among Nigerian people as a whole.

Since there seems to be some pride and normalcy in absurdity, which has received a standing ovation in America lately, I decided to put in my two pence in the bowl of the ridicule. Ironically somebody might have the courage to single me out as an odd man out. At the end of this book, I introduced to Congress and anyone who may be listening, my own Bill Of Rights for the Nation. I'm only trying to belong. My Bill of Rights is modeled on some of the Constitution, some of the Amendments and a bunch of the Congressional laws guiding our Country for over two hundred years. Some of the interpretations of the Amendments and Congressional laws are more interesting and perhaps, troubling. Worse still are the interpretations of Activist Judges with regard to these laws. But if some people recognize some oddities in my Bill of Rights, they should be patient with me. Or may be they should revisit all of our existing laws. It might, just might make someone to muster the courage to call on their Representatives and Senators in Washington D. C., all the Lawmakers in the fifty States to review the Amendments and Congressional laws and State laws in the United States of America. We think this is a Congressional and State Assembly duties that are actually over due. Right now they are on borrowed time, our time.

CHAPTER ONE:
THE MARRIAGE

From the way America and Nigeria interact politically, socially and economically today, one would think that the relationship had been there for ever. But in actual fact the Nigerian-American marriage is only a few Decades old. There was even no courtship before the eventual marriage, which was based strictly on economic and strategic interests, the balance of which could be the subject of a whole other story. It can be argued however, that Nigeria, at one time, directly or indirectly, had something to do with America by way of the infamous slave trade. But that relationship is not one of pride or dignity. But it was a relationship all the same; a historical fact, which cannot be denied.

The real and long relationship that Nigeria has had was with Great Britain. In a very real and strict sense, it was Great Britain which "created" the territory called Nigeria as it is today. Nigeria was one of the Colonial Satellites of Britain for 46 years 10 months – (two months shy of 47 years- from January 1, 1914 to October 1, 1960). As early as 1877, an Englishman, George Goldie (1846-1925) set out with his brother to explore the interior of Nigeria. That trip was cut short because his brother caught a very dangerous fever on the Nile River. Mr. Goldie had brought the entire West Coast under England's control. There was intensive trading going on along the Coast and the Niger River. Many British trading companies were operating mostly in Lagos and Niger Delta area. When the English Government found that there were other countries interested in the area, she decided to go to the hinterland and take complete possession of the area. This was the time in history popularly known as "the scramble for Africa". Great Britain sent a military officer, Lord Fredrick Luggard to consolidate the British interest in Northern and Southern Protectorates of the Territory hunted down by Mr. George Goldie, "the Founder of Nigeria". At the suggestion of an English lady journalist, Flora Shaw, whom he later married, Goldie named this Territory "Niger Area" (the area along the Niger). Eventually this area came to be known as NIGERIA. Without going deep into the different stages of the amalgamation process of the Northern and Southern Protectorates, Nigeria became a unified entity under British rule with all the implications of colonization, of which some are good, and some are bad. Today Nigeria has about 240 language groups because the British Government's need for a big territory took precedence over a homogeneous entity with one or two languages. Thus over two hundred tribes were forced together as a people by a foreign power.

The relationship between Britain and Nigeria became that of Master and Servant. While Great Britain was a very powerful and developed country, Nigeria was a very undeveloped and uneducated as far as Western education was concerned. One of the first things the British Government did was to establish schools to teach the people how to read and write. The Nigerian–British relationship proper began in 1914. But the educational system put in place by the British for Nigerians was not primarily for the benefit of the Nigerian people. Instead the colonial masters intended that a very few Nigerians should receive education in order to communicate with the "masters" for the good of the "masters" only. Hence the core curriculum of the first educational system was for the "study of English" in order to turn out interpreters for the white man and some people to do domestic work for the "white man".

In 1934, after 20 years, Yaba College of Education, the first institution of higher learning was established to train students to work in the Civil Service of colonized Nigeria. The natives were needed in the Nigerian Civil Service. At the completion of their studies, the Yaba College of Education graduates received diploma certificates in Arts, economics, agriculture, engineering or medicine, just diploma certificates. But these certificates were not backed up by any University because Yaba College of Education was not affiliated to any British University. That would mean that Yaba College of Education graduates would be subordinate and inferior to British officials doing the same jobs in Nigeria. This state of affairs was not quite welcome by some Nigerian semi-elites at the time. These semi-elites could see that Nigerians with Yaba College of Education diplomas would never attain a position of leadership in the Civil Service sector. Consequently about 1934 the Nigerian Youth Movement (NYM) was born to address issues they see as discrimination. This was the first multi-ethnic organization in Nigeria up to this time. Even before the establishment of Yaba College of Education, the Nigerian Youth Movement had organized a strong mass rally to protest the establishment of the College. While the Movement did not stop the building of the College, it constantly turned the heat on the government through anti-colonial rallies and protests. In their manifesto the Nigerian Youth Movement demanded that there be an aggressive education policy for every Nigerian child and equal economic opportunity for every Nigerian youth. The membership of the Nigerian Youth Movement grew fast. It became a very powerful organ of protest and change. This Movement formed the Nigerian National Democratic Party. One of the prominent members of NYM was Benjamin Nnamdi Azikiwe, who joined the Movement in 1937. He served in the Executive Council of the movement. In the same year Nnamdi Azikiwe established a newspaper called the West African Pilot, which was a big success. The newspaper enjoyed a wide audience even in neighboring West African countries. It goes without saying that the newspaper was very anti Colonial Britain. It took until 1948 before the educational aspirations of the Nigerian Youth Movement began to bear fruit. The British Administrative Governor of Nigeria, Sir John Mac-Pherson, established a University College in Ibadan in 1948, but it was not affiliated to the University of London. That, however, took about 34 years to come about. This University College was purely for Arts, no Sciences. The Colonial

Masters felt a need for Arts graduates in the work force for the good of the economy and eventually for their own good.

In the thirties and forties some freedom seekers from Nigeria and Gold Coast (Ghana) decided to study in America. Long before the Nigerian struggle, there had been a far more serious struggle in the United States of America. A Jamaican by the name Marcus Garvey moved into America in 1916. With the help of the freedom of expression in America, he created a formidable and mass movement with the hope of uniting all blacks into one independent nation. He held conventions attended by delegates from Africa. Marcus had a very grandiose plan for all black peoples of the world. He established the "Black Star Shipping Line" operating from America to Africa in order to encourage blacks in the Americas to return to Mother Africa to fight for their Freedom and Independence as a Nation. He also had a journal called "the Negro World", which was widely read in Africa. In 1920 a branch of the Marcus Garvey Movement, "the Universal Negro Improvement Association", was established in Lagos. "The Negro World" was eagerly waited for in Lagos by subscribers. This newspaper was the organ of his propaganda. In one of the Conventions Mr. Garvey was chosen as the provisional President of Africa Nation. The group had chosen a National Flag and Anthem for Africa. Marcus was ready to use violence to achieve his goal of a Negro State made up of ex-African slaves and Africans on the Continent. A quasi Nigerian-American relationship was about to begin. But this relationship was not governmental in nature.

The grandiose aspirations of Marcus were cut short when he was arrested, jailed and later deported from the United States of America back to Jamaica. His movement collapsed; but his political philosophy did not completely die. He had a lot of converts in Africa and elsewhere. His ideas set fire on some Nigerians. Nnamdi Azikiwe was one of his adherents. In those days it was an act of rebellion for a Nigerian to study in America instead of Great Britain. "Zik", as he was popularly called, was one of the few "rebels", who had the courage to secure admission into an American university. He attended an almost all black college. As a poor Nigerian student he saw discrimination and protests by African American organizations first hand and on a regular basis. Zik got two American Masters degrees, which were not recognized in his own Country, Nigeria, under the British rule. Consequently he left Nigeria for Gold Coast now Ghana and established the "Accra Morning Post" newspaper. He also published his first book "Renascent Africa". In the Gold Coast Nnamdi Azikiwe got into trouble with authorities and he returned to Nigeria, where instead of seeking civil service work again, became a journalist and a nationalist of no mean stature. He made very good use of his newspaper, West African Pilot and put into action what he learnt from Marcus and African American civil rights protests during his student days in the United States of America. What he saw before him in Nigeria was a repeat of the white discrimination and oppression of blacks in America. It turned out that Nnamdi Azikiwe, who, because he studied in the United States of America, could not get a civil service job in his own country with two Masters Degrees from America, became one of the Indigenous Founding Fathers of Independent Nigeria and her first President in a Parliamentary System of Government. After the Nigerian Independence on October 1, 1960, power shifted from the British Colonials to the Indigenous Nigerians. In like manner goods and services from the United States of America were no longer regarded as inferior. This change of attitude did not happen overnight with a people who had been taught for 46 years to dislike and despise Americans, American goods and American University degrees. Of course while this was happening, the Nigerian public scarcely knew that the antagonism between America and Britain was a part of the British-American politics borne out of the American Independence from Britain after a fierce war between them. America won her independence on the battle field.

With the help of Nigerians like Zik, who studied in America, some degree of trade and other relationships started between Nigeria and America from the sixties. During the Civil war, the Nigerian side maintained some level of relationship with the American Government. On May 16, 1967, a United States' Senator in a public statement said:

"The U. S. has already intervened repeatedly in the area: first by propping up general Gowon when he assumed power, later by backing him when Nigeria abrogated the Aburi agreement (the product of negotiation between Gowon and Ojukwu on the terms of federation, which Gowon promptly disregarded at the instance of British diplomats, who felt that he had made too many concessions to eastern/Ibo regionalism); and also by exerting pressure on a matter of African nations not to recognize Biafra." Also in a letter to the Nigerian American Chamber of Commerce in Lagos, the United States Ambassador to Nigeria, Elbert Matthews, wrote immediately the Nigerian Biafra war began:

"The fact is simple. My government recognizes the federal military government as the government of Nigeria. We have repeatedly made known our complete support of political integrity (sic) of Nigeria. Many times we have expressed our hopes that Nigeria would continue to remain a united country. This is not only an official view, but one that is also felt by American businessmen engaged in the rapidly growing trade between our two countries."

(Daily Times of Nigeria Newspaper –Lagos 27th July, 1967)

Today there are probably over 165,000 Nigerians in the U. S. So much has happened since 1967.

As a result of the new Nigerian Government, many Nigerians started to attend American Universities in the seventies and eighties. The Nigerian economy was at its peak. The Nigerian Naira was then more valuable than the American dollar. In 1979, one dollar ($1.00) was equivalent to 67 kobo (0.67 Naira). (100 kobo make 1 Naira as 100 pennies make one dollar) More than half of the Nigerian Universities now are staffed by Americans and American trained Lecturers and Professors. Many of the High Schools in Nigeria in the sixties were influenced by the presence of "American Peace Corps Program" put in place under the John F. Kennedy Administration in the early sixties. After the Military regimes in Nigeria, one of the dilemmas she faced was the form of Government to be adopted by the incoming Civilian Government. Nigerians, influenced by the so many American trained political operatives, decided to go from the British Parliamentary system of Government to the American Presidential system of Government, which is still the form of Government operating in Nigeria today. The Nigerian-American marriage relationship was taking shape. Gradually Nigeria started to disengage from Britain and get closer and closer to America. After all both Nigeria and the United States of America were British Colonies at one point in their history; Nigeria for 46 plus years (1914 -1960) and the United States of America for 124 years (1651-1775). That was not all; Nigeria had recently discovered liquid "gold" (Crude Oil) in a great quantity. The number of her suitors increased and the intensity of the pursuit increased too. American made goods, which were banned as inferior goods under the British era, started to flow into the Nigerian market.

Part of the concern of this writer is how well this marriage will serve Nigeria. Was it a wise decision to file a divorce in the Nigerian-British marriage regardless of the inequality of the relationship? Will the new marriage with the United States of America be any better morally, socially and economically? Nigeria is now the third or fourth largest supplier of crude oil to the United States of America and the Nigerian Crude Oil is one of the best on the market. What is the greatest export of America to Nigeria? That is the question. Hopefully it is not an exportation of "freedom" American style. This writer is concerned because of the adverse effects that the misinterpretation and abuse of freedom have brought on the American people since the sixties.

The enjoyment of modern technologies in the United States of America is instantaneously experienced in Nigeria. The Cable News Network (CNN), BTN etc are clearly seen live in Nigeria as they broadcast in the United States of America. The life style in America is instinctively copied by people in Nigeria. "The Soul Train" re-run is a constant feature on some Nigerian Television Stations. In short Nigerians have become participants in almost every event in America as the world shrinks in the face of technological advancements. In some instances it is good; but in some it is not so good. The latter is the point of our discussion and evaluation in this book. Is Nigeria ready to "drink the chalice that America is drinking" right now? That is another question. Unfortunately it is a bitter drink, which many are getting tired of.

As was noted earlier, there are many Americans and American Businesses and American trained lecturers in Nigeria and the Nigerian school system. Through the influence of these American trained teachers, many policy statements in the Nigerian schools today were copied straight from the American school system. Under the British rule schools had the long vacation during the dry months of the year. But when the American influence came on the scene, schools long vacation changed to American summer months, which is rainy season in Nigeria. Consequently Nigerian students, even today do not enjoy their vacation because of the heavy rains of May, June July, August and September.

Under the British era in Nigeria, promotion was based on strict student performance and merit; but through the influence of American trained Federal Ministers of Education and State Commissioners of Education and their advisers, students' promotion from one class to the next became automatic just as it has been in America. At some point there was a move in Nigeria to change the long vacation back to the dry season. The bad effect of automatic promotion is still lingering in the Nigerian educational system today. There was no incentive for student learning since everybody was sure of being shuffled to the next class the next year irrespective of whether or not the students can read, write, add, multiply and subtract. The regrettable consequence is that Nigerian schools produced a lot of unschooled and uneducated High School graduates, who could not pass West African School Certificate Examinations (WASC) or the General Certificate of Education (GCE) Examinations. Many of such High School graduates cannot qualify to enter any Universities in Nigeria or abroad. This inadequacy resulted in the establishment of "remedial schools" in many universities and other schools of higher learning in the country to remedy the situation and prepare students for institutions of Higher Learning in the Country and abroad. The ripple effect of this educational copycatting in the Nigerian educational system has caused the devaluation of Nigerian education. It put a very serious damp on the spirit of healthy competitive spirit in the Nigerian students. Instead what Nigeria had was a mass production of "educated illiterates", who are not employable in any good paying jobs in the Nigerian job market. Mass class promotion had exactly the same adverse effects in Nigeria as it has had on the American society but to a lesser degree. But because of her two hundred plus years of existence, high technological advancement and dollar power,

America could adjust better in the face of the mistakes made in the school system by mass promotion than Nigeria ever could. Even with the establishment of Community Colleges to rehabilitate High School drop-outs in the American experience, there are still a good number of pure illiterates in a country where Elementary and High Schools are completely free. The lingering effects of this mistake in American educational system are still enormous. For instance, America still has the record in the number of incarcerated citizens in the world. The statistics put the number of Americans in prison at 2,131,180 as of 2005. Again a good number of inmates in American prisons are elementary or high schools dropouts. Of course the other reasons for the high inmate population are the recent interpretations of "Freedom", the lowering of moral values and the destruction of the American family. Unless Nigeria is very careful in the way and manner she copies from the American culture, she will run the risk of plunging herself into the very deep waters, which America is now finding difficult to climb out. If it has been so difficult for America to get a handle on illiteracy and its attendant problems, how much more would such a trend be difficult to combat in Nigerian? As in America many of the trouble makers in Nigeria are Elementary and High school drop-outs. Everybody wants a good life. But without the training and education to back it up, young Nigerians, who like to live "big" anyway, turn to illegal means to make a living through armed robbery, and "419" fraud scheme of all descriptions. The Bush Administration is trying very hard to correct the mistake by implementing the "no child left behind" program. In the Bill signed by the President, accountability and measurement in the classroom were the highlights just as it used to be many years ago in Britain, Nigeria and America. He told educators that if a child did not pass the examinations, he or she should not be promoted. Instead the child should be put in a remedial class until that student could learn the subject matter. It is our hope that the Nigerian Ambassador in the United States is taking note. The mass promotion policy in Nigeria must be rescinded as the first step toward Nigerian educational recovery. It wasn't so in the beginning. In the twenties, thirties, forties and fifties in America and in the thirties, forties, fifties and sixties in Nigeria, the standard of education was much higher than now. A grade school student then would read and write, add and subtract and comprehend better than a High School student of today both in Nigeria and America.

Life in America in the thirties, forties and fifties was simple and enjoyable because people were family oriented, friendly and God fearing. They understood the Holy Book, which tells us: "The fear of the Lord is the beginning of wisdom". There were rules and regulations. People could immediately recognize the good from the bad, identify a man from a woman a mile away. Truth was not relative but absolute and unchanging. "Honor your father and your mother" was still the fourth Commandment and was taken seriously. People gave respect and expected and received respect too. There was respect for life and property for most Americans. At that time, any deviation from the standard of morality was an exception frowned at by the generality of the American people. What went wrong with the American society could easily go wrong with the Nigerian society too unless....

Chapter Two:

The Age of Rebellion

The period of the sixties was morally a very troubled period in the American history. A modern liberal Democrat was in the White House. The Viet Nam War was raging. While some Americans were fighting and dying at the hands of the North Viet Nam soldiers, some unpatriotic Americans were in North Viet Nam criticizing their Government and their soldiers in combat. On the streets of American cities there were anti Viet Nam War demonstrations. Dissent and American Flag burning on the streets of America were common scenes. Most of the societal problems of today seem to have been born in this period. The sixties became known as "the age of the 'Hippie' culture", "the sexual revolution age", "the Woodstock age", "the do your own thing age", "the anything goes age", "the feel good age", the "everybody is doing it age", "the Viet Nam unpopular war age", "the free love age", and the "I'm alright, you're alright, we're alright" age. Behind these ideologies came moral relativism, which says that if one thinks an action is okay, it is okay. No action is good or bad until the individual says it is good or bad. In other words, one can make a number of assumptions based on the thesis that nothing is good or bad. One could then say that pre-meditated murder may be fine if one thinks it is fine. You could go about raping women and molesting children if you think it is okay. One could in clear conscience rob a bank every week, commit abortion every three months or one could practically do anything one wants to do and it would be perfectly fine. There would absolutely be nothing morally wrong about individuals with this kind of mindset. From this false philosophy the popular saying: "I'm okay; you are okay; we are okay, everybody is okay", came into the American society. That philosophy posits the idea that there is no standard to judge anything or anyone from, since the morality of every action is subjective. There is no such thing as "a good" or "bad" conduct. The purpose of this philosophy is to eliminate conscience, guilt and sin because "you are okay; and I'm okay"; "don't tell and I won't tell". If I feel like blowing up a stadium full of a couple thousands of people, it would be morally fine if I think it is fine to do so. Does that sound familiar? The same argument should go for any other "crime" for which society throws people into prison or jail. Many people fed with the relativity philosophy still don't believe in prison or punishment. These people form the center of all protests and anti-morality activism going on today in America. Unfortunately many from this generation, are part of the political system now and that raises very serious problems for some American politicians today, because they carried over a lot of the attitudes of the sixties. If actions are relative, why do we have a justice system? Should we have a justice system at all? Why are some people in jails and prisons today, if people make and follow only their own laws? Do you see any contradictions already in the system, which is defending moral relativism and at the same time putting people in jails and prisons? The idea of justice itself runs into a big problem because it would be very difficult to do justice in a system that operates on relativism. Even though there is no explicit and official law pointing to relativism, there are implicit laws and interpretations of existing laws, which point to and endorse relativism.

It is the crazy sixties, which has defined the America we have today. Many of the "who is who" in America today: political leaders, influential journalists, university professors and lecturers, economists, entrepreneurs and, in fact all the baby-boomers are all products of the sixties. The majority of our law makers and Executives in State Houses all over the country is either the product of this era or has been trained or raised by them. Is there any real surprise then in the way this country lines up now morally? Everything seems to be according to the script. Exactly! It is manifested in the laws, the dress code, music, religious practice, religious vocations, murder averages, co-habitations, marriages and divorces, justice systems, pornographic industries, thefts, educational systems, movies and dangerous drugs use. The old, the normal, the constant are described as "conservative" and therefore bad and should be discarded, even in the Church. From the sixties to the present, things have tended to go south naturally and with ease. There didn't need to be any prodding for people to go heading south. Those who could do something about it are few, silent or undisturbed precisely because it is "not politically correct"; many of those who are talking about it lack the power to do anything about it because they have no political cloud; they are numerically small. That sounds like the beginning of an end to me.

In the sixties women threw away the long skirts and picked up the mini dress. The men grew long and wild hair. In many cases men looked like women. Norms and standard protocols in the American dress culture were discarded. To wear ones pants inside out would no longer look odd. Instead it would be "cool". We are still living today with the vestiges of that era. Teenage boys sweeping the streets with their dropping (falling off) pants as they walk, is still a regular street scene and occurrence. That they expose their underwear would not look awkward at all. To wear a T-shirt, which is twice bigger and longer than the outer shirt is seen as cool. This is considered being in fashion. Among teenage girls and some adult women too, showing off their bellybuttons by wearing very short blouses, becomes a fashion statement of its own. It is not worth mentioning here what Hollywood ladies wear during the Oscars and Emmys. That is off the chart of indecency.

Drinking excessive alcohol, smoking, snuffing and injecting dangerous drugs, all of which were signs of rebellion and revolution for the sixties' youths, have become popular among young people today. That combination resulted in excessive and inordinate sexual activities and behaviors then and now. Unwanted pregnancies, which are natural results of those behaviors, became common place in the sixties just as it is today. Resorting to contraceptives to stop pregnancies led to carelessness and promiscuity, which in turn caused more pregnancies and more abortions. Their inordinate desire for the abortion of these innocent babies during the sixties paved the way for the 1973 Roe versus Wade Supreme Court decision that legalized abortion on demand in the United States of America. That decision put the icing on the immorality cake of the Nation. Since then the assault on unborn babies has been relentless for a few weeks old babies to seven, eight and almost nine months old in the case of "partial birth" abortions.

On the Nigerian theatre the picture was different in the sixties. The traditional Nigerian was surrounded by a lot of cultural taboos that had very strict rules. The religious beliefs (indigenous and foreign, Moslem and Christian) were very strong in the sixties. The family ties and structures constituted the checks and balances in the morality of the Nigerian society. There was a tremendous strength in the "extended family system", which connected many individuals and families into one "big family", which can be called village or clan. Invariably each village is supposed to be made up of people from one man and one woman or many wives in a polygamous family (before the advent of Christianity). That is why there is no inter-marriage within such a village no matter how big it becomes. Family values were real and operational. Everyone in the extended family system was helped and helpful as well as respected and respectful to one another. There were duties and obligations on everyone, young and old. The raising of children was not completely left to the biological parents. It was the responsibility of everyone who had anything to contribute. If an adult saw a child or teen doing what he was not supposed to do, that adult had the right and obligation to correct the child as if he or she was the biological parent for the common good of the community. The biological parents would be happy and thankful that their child was corrected by a neighbor and would do the same for another family if the situation arose. It exemplified the Biblical phrase "being my brother's keeper".

Elders played a very big role in maintaining discipline and order in the community. Crimes, though rare, were abhorred and dealt with promptly by the Elders, who dispensed justice without fear or favor. They were aware of the consequences on themselves as individuals and on the community at large if they played with justice. Their guiding principle was always the Supreme Being. Irrespective of the tribe, culture or the religious group one is talking about in

Nigeria, these principles were similar or the same. It should be mentioned here that Nigeria has over two hundred language and cultural groups. These taboos and laws constituted what we would now call the Constitution or, in Christian terminology, the Ten Commandments of the natives. In the traditional Igbo society (one of the language groups), for example, if there was a crime of incest, the culprit would be ostracized from the society. Then the culprit would perform some sacrificial atonement to the deity before he could be received back into association with the community. The unborn baby was, of course, sacred and abortion was not an option. The fear now is: how much of this tradition is still in tact in the Nigerian society today in the midst of associations and marriages with other foreign cultures like the United States of America? Has Nigeria not been introduced to the sexual revolution, abortion and divorce cultures by the so-called educated elites? How many American Government and Private Foundations are now sponsoring "family planning" and contraceptive clinics in Nigeria? Nigeria is not quite insulated from the moral erosion anymore. Things are changing already and fast too.

While the Nigerian society is not quite over the edge yet, it is on the way. Hence there is a need for this write-up. There is a constant and relentless attack on some of the old cultures as described above by the so-called elites and progressives, who studied in the United States of America and other parts of Europe. This attack is more on some parts of the country and less on others. The Muslim North is not as fast catching on as the Christian South is. The battle has been on since the seventies, about ten years after the American moral revolution of the sixties started and some years after the end of the Nigerian civil war. Incidentally that was when the Nigerian Government and the American Government started going steady for the eventual marriage. Crude oil started to flow in the seventies and the "almighty" dollar started to change hands. Since then many other things have exchanged hands too, the good, the bad and the ugly. Nigeria is not quite down yet in a lot of areas but the jury is still out.

The strong religious upbringing of the Nigerian equivalent of the American Baby Boomers is the only cork holding the gin in the bottle up to now. But the last group of that generation has got one foot in the grave already. And that is a concern. There are still some men and women of that generation in Government now putting a damp on the fast approaching "storm". But the clock is ticking. The awareness of these facts makes it urgent for Nigerians to step back and check and recheck what they learn and import from abroad, especially the United States of America. Nigeria should learn from the mistakes of countries around North America. The evidence is in what has happened to the third-world American neighbors to the South, who are morally confused as it is now. They are born into religion but most of them do not know the rudiments of their religion. Consequently there is a lot of external religion going on, but no interiorizing and deepening of the faith. The result is massive confusion of individuals, who are between two conflicting values, one Mexican, for instance, one American. It would be a very big mistake for Nigeria to brush aside this awareness as unimportant. Some would be blinded and think that, since America is now the only super power in the world, everything from America would be the best and the right way to go. It may be the way to go; but the way to go where? It must be recalled that so many Empires had come and gone. Any created person that has attempted to take the place of God at any time in history has failed. Great Empires and Civilizations had piqued with power and arrogance and fallen because their arrogance blinded them from seeing God, the Author of everything. Can we forget the Babylonian Empire and Civilization, Ancient Egyptian Civilization, the Roman Empire and Civilization, the British Empire and Civilization, the German Empire in the making under Hitler, and the Russian Empire of "yesterday". To a large extent these are now prominent only on the pages of history books. While there may not be any outside power to defeat America, her greatest instruments of failure and eventual demise will come from within because of what is happening now within her if left unchecked. Unfortunately the internal erosion has gone so deep that it would need a strong moral revolution to check the impending disaster. It would take a Moral Rearmament five times stronger than the sexual revolution of the sixties, which set the Nation on a downward spiral, to stir the Nation aright. If the giant that is America has the potential of collapse, guess what can and will happen to American satellites like Nigeria. For

Nigeria this is the acceptable time to step back and recapture her rich heritage, drop what is negative from her past, reject unproductive imported cultures, and forge a workable proposition, which will blend the best of the two or more cultures. If this opportunity is lost, the children of the present bad elements in Nigeria will take lawlessness and immorality to a whole new level unprecedented in the Nigerian short history. The seeds of corruption, indiscipline and lack of the fear of God are gradually germinating and digging in with the help of media and advancing technologies. But once the young trees get well grounded, they will begin to bear worse and more formidable fruits unless they are uprooted immediately. Now is the time. Nigeria has been saturated with a lot of these seeds; many have germinated ready to grow and produce. It is not too late to get rid of these bad seeds because they are not many and are not quite deep rooted yet. Unlike America, Nigeria is not over the edge yet and has a strong cultural heritage to stop the advance of the new and imported amoral revolution. That could be good news for Nigeria only if some political and religious changes are made now to teach the children the values, which their grand parents lost at the advent of foreign cultures' intervention. If you think that Nigerian coup and counter coups, bribery and corruption in low and high places, indiscipline and greed, armed robbery and "419", hunger and suffering are rampant in the Nigerian society of today, wait till the next generation takes over the affairs of State and governance. America is still hanging on, in spite of very serious moral problem because she has a sophisticated and high technology plus more than two hundred years of history to manage the effects of these moral problems like crimes, Aids and a host of others. Without her technological superiority to combat crimes, for instance, the country would have been a war zone more than it is at the moment. America has other things going for her: the natural demarcations of the country make her a very huge Island; and the political design of the American politics and its huge size make it very difficult to carry out or stage a successful "coup d'etat" in the United States. That is an advantage, which Nigeria does not have. But even then it is only prolonging the inevitable unless there is a change of heart in the United States of America. But does anyone know what really went wrong in the U. S. of A.?

CHAPTER THREE:

THE AMERICAN CONSTITUTION

A Constitution, any constitution at all, is a system of laws or body of fundamental rules and principles of a Nation, State, Group, or body politic, which determines the powers and duties of Government or those in charge of the group and guarantees certain rights and obligations to the people in that country, state or group. It is the mode in which a State or Society is organized and operated. It can be said to be the sum total of what a group or a nation is about. It becomes the point of reference and a guide to rule and govern the group or nation. A Constitution, therefore, is not static; it can be changed or improved upon. The body which puts the Constitution together can and do add or remove parts or a whole section from the Constitution if it goes to help the management of the people or group better. Some Constitutions are written down; some are not. While some Constitutions are produced at the creation of the group or nation, others are formed as the group or nation grows as a body.

In a Presidential System such as United States and Nigeria there are, for instance, a set of laws made before the Government is even formed. The Constitution stipulates the way to form a Government and the two Houses of the Senate and Representatives which will make further laws to govern the people with as the nation progresses. The Parliamentary System, on the other hand has the House of Lords and the House of Commons which make laws as they go. These representatives of the people make laws, which, if signed by the Executive, the President or the Prime Minister, become part of the Constitution. That is why a Constitution can be said to be a dynamic document. The Constitution of a nation is designed to be interpreted by the Judicial Branch as an impartial judge. But unfortunately judges, who are supposed to interpret the laws, are not always free from partisan politics or personal agenda. In a Presidential System like the United States or Nigeria, the governance of the country is the responsibility of the three branches of Government: The Executive Branch (President, who executes and makes things happen), The Legislative Branch (the law makers) and The Judicial Branch (the interpreters of the law). This is to make sure that one branch does not dominate or hijack the entire direction of a country. The maintenance of the governmental fairness equilibrium is called "checks and balances". When the Lawmakers send a bill to the President it does not become part of the constitution until the President signs it. By this device, neither the Legislators nor the President can interpret laws, while the Justices do not make or execute decisions. But unfortunately some judges fall into the temptation of "legislating" from the bench in the name of interpretation of the law. This is judicial activism, which is unconstitutional because the Framers of the American Constitution separated the three powers of government very well. The Judges' job is to interpret existing laws not make new ones. But if they think some laws need to be updated or changed, they could kick it back to the Law Makers to do something with it. That is the way that the sanctity of the system is preserved.

Before the drafting and adoption of the Constitution the thirteen Colonies declared their Independence from Britain. In that declaration the representatives of the Colonies wrote:

"We hold these truths to be self-evident, that all men are created equal, that they are endowed by their Creator with certain unalienable Rights that among these are life, Liberty and pursuit of Happiness...."

The general statement by the Founders sets the tone of the New Nation in the making – namely that all men are created equal by God; no one created himself and no one should lord it over other people; that God has a place in the lives of the people of this new nation; that we do not need to be rocket scientists to know these truths because they are self-evident; that some of these rights are respect for life, freedom and happiness. This should be a reminder to all the Justices and members of Congress about the mind of the Founding Fathers with regard to these United States of America.

THE PREAMBLE:

This is the preamble to the Constitution of the United States of America. For our purpose here we are going to leave the Seven Articles alone and go straight to the Amendments, which came after the Constitution was written. The first ten Amendments were adopted June 15, 1790. The rest were adopted at different times by different Congresses over the years. It reads:

"We the people of the United States, in order to form a more perfect union, establish justice, insure domestic tranquility, provide for the common defense, promote the general welfare, and secure the blessings of liberty to ourselves and our posterity, do ordain and establish this Constitution for the United States of America."

Now let us examine just the First Amendment.

THE FIRST AMENDMENT OF THE AMERICAN CONSTITUTION:

Congress shall make no law respecting an establishment of religion, or prohibiting the free exercise thereof; or abridging the freedom of speech or of the press; or the right of the people peaceably to assemble and petition the Government for a redress of grievances.

The first Amendment guarantees all Americans free exercise of religion, freedom of speech and press and the right of assembly and the right of the people to petition for any grievances that need attention.

1. Congress shall make no law respecting an establishment of religion:

The operative word here is **establishment.** To establish in this context means: To cause to be recognized and accepted; to found; to make a State institution of (Church). Establishment means: The act of establishing; the fact or state of being established; as in an established Church.

A State established religion enjoys the power of the State. That means that the State will enforce the obligation on the members of the State to practice that and no other religion.

For the Founding Fathers, this non establishment of a state religion and free exercise of religion clauses were probably the most important in the First Amendment because they were all men of religion and were perhaps personally persecuted in the 'Old Country' or in the British Colonies, of which American States formed a collection of those Colonies. Based on the experiences of the Founding Fathers in Europe and the American Colonies, it was a very good safe-guard to enshrine in the laws to guide this young Nation the freedom to worship the way each person saw fit. The religion of the king is the religion of the people, ("Cuius Regio, eius religio") was a very common practice in Europe before America was born. In this doctrine every subject was forced to practice the religion of the king. That is the background in which "congress shall make no laws respecting the establishment of religion" was born. The immigrants from Europe to America were familiar with the persecution, which accompanied that doctrine. Some of them left Europe to escape persecution there by coming to the new land – America. The Founding Fathers did not like the idea of a State-run-religion in the United States of America. They clearly understood that the United States was made up of many colonies and of diverse peoples with different religious backgrounds. Invariably most of the 13 American Colonies were established by people who were looking for religious freedom of one kind or another. For instance, there were the Anglicans in Jamestown, the Pilgrims at Plymouth, the Puritans at Massachusetts Bay, the Catholics in Maryland, and the Quakers in Pennsylvania. Since they wanted everyone to be happy in the New Land, the freedom of religion clause was very appropriate and vital.

Let us examine this piece of legislation a little more closely. Off the top, the idea of a Monarch in the United States was another 'no' 'no' issue. The Founding Fathers wanted a government in which the people would have a say; they did not want to be ruled by the whims and mood swings of a Monarch. When these States were just Colonies under the British rule, there was no American representation in the British Parliament. The Colonists paid taxes but they did not have any say as to how the money was used. The Colonists resented and fought against "taxation without representation". It was no surprise then that the first American Congress wanted the "Government of the people, for the people and by the people." The first thing they did was to let the power to make laws rest on Congress elected by the people. The Founding Fathers went on to say that **not even** Congress has the power **to establish a State religion**. Even if ninety percent of Congress were of one particular religion, they could not vote to make it **the religion of the land** without violating the Constitution. That means that the issue of establishing a religion was out of the question and rightly so. Where then did ACLU and the Federal Supreme Court come up with the idea that school prayer violates the First Amendment since ordinary prayer by students is not and could not be an establishment of religion? The First Amendment said that the government had no right to establish a **State religion**. It did not say that citizens should not practice their religion anywhere they choose. It did not stipulate any place to pray. On the contrary, it said that the government should not stop people from the exercise of their religion.

2. Or prohibiting the free exercise thereof;

To make sure that everyone understood that religion was important, the Founding Fathers said that there should be no prohibition on the practice of religion of individuals or groups of citizens. Not even Congress has the power to prevent people from doing their duty to their God the way and the place they choose, (First Amendment). It must be realized that the Founding Fathers were religious people themselves, who wanted to feel free to worship God. The Framers of this Constitution were being defended by the Justices when they said in article 111 of Northwest Ordinance, July 13, 1787: "Religion, morality, and knowledge being necessary to good government and the happiness of mankind, schools and the means of education shall forever be encouraged." This was re-ratified on September 25,

1789, the same day that the same Congress approved the wordings of the First Amendment. Looking at the incongruity of the so-called unconstitutionality of school prayer by the Supreme Court, the author of THE MYTH OF SEPARATION, David Barton, said: "Since both (referring to the two documents mentioned above) were approved on the same day, it is evident that our Founders did not believe that establishing a frame of government mandating that religion, morality, and knowledge be provided through schools was a violation of the First Amendment prohibition on the establishment of religion". David Barton is perfectly right. The Founding Fathers did not intend the First Amendment to produce students without religion or moral principles. Instead they prescribed religion as part of the school in order to produce good citizens. Abraham Lincoln, the 16th President of the United States of America said that the only assurance of our nation's safety is to lay our foundation in morality and religion. There is some evidence to show that the Founders of our nation wanted religion in school. The first schools were founded to teach people how to read the Bible. The first American College, Harvard, required that "every student be plainly instructed and earnestly pressed to consider well the main end of his life and studies is to know God and Jesus Christ which is eternal life, John.17: 3, and therefore to lay Christ in the bottom, as the foundation of all sound knowledge and learning." Students were required to read the Bible two times a day. This was legal and the motto of Harvard University was: "For Christ and the Church". For a long time religious tolerance as part of the Constitution was inviolate and sacrosanct. But recently this Constitutional protection has been challenged by some individuals and the American Civil Liberties Union (ACLU). In recent history, we have the Mc Collum v. Board of Education, Religion taught in Public School: (1948); the Engel v. Vitale (1962) Called School Prayer Decision; the School District of Abington Township v. schempp Bible Reading Case: (1963) ; Wisconsin v. Yoder; The Case of the Amish Children: (1972) and Lee v. Weisman (1992. Gradually these and others have been making some inroads into the dismantling of God and worship of God in this Nation, which was founded "under God". The tragedy of the success of ACLU is that the courts, which are supposed to interpret and defend the Constitution, have instead gone into the business of making laws and thereby advancing the ACLU agenda. To legislate from the bench is, of course, unconstitutional. But who is going to stop judges from legislating from the bench? Thank God some of their fellow judges do try through "dissent". Judges are not supposed to be activists or advocates because they do not have clients, or shall we say, "not supposed to have clients"; they are supposed to be referees, who interpret the Constitution without fear or favor. The majority of Judges in the Federal Supreme Court, the highest court in the land, ruled that it is unconstitutional for children to say prayers out loud in school. By it, students are not allowed, even on their own, to say their prayers in school. They say that it violates the Constitution for students to say prayers on school grounds, even during recess or lunch. That is ridiculous to image that the Supreme Court would make such a judgment. If School prayer is unconstitutional, why is it constitutional for *PLANNED PARENTHOOD* to distribute condoms, books and magazines that promote sexual activity among minors without parental permission in Public Schools? Some of the books that they have distributed are "Boys and Sex" and "Girls and Sex". You might say what is wrong with that? Let us go inside these books.

Here we go: From "BOYS AND SEX", read on:
"...More and more people are coming to understand that having sex is a joyful and enriching experience at any age." (Page 2.)
"...playing with girls sexually before adolescence ...increases the chances for a satisfactory sex life when a boy grows up." (page 38.)
Premarital intercourse does have its definite values as a training ground for marriage...boys and girls who start having intercourse when they're adolescents...will find that it's a big help...it's like taking a car out on a test run before you buy it."(page 117)
"Premarital intercourse among adolescents is often helpful in later life because it's easier to learn things in our earlier years." (page118)

From "GIRLS AND SEX", we read:
"...Everyone's agreed...that teenage sex should be a learning experience. (page 15)
"Sex play with boys...can be exciting, pleasurable, and even worthwhile...it will help later sexual adjustment." (page 48)

The above quotes were taken from: The Myth of Separation: by David Barton.

Is this the kind of material that parents want the Public School to give their teens in a society, where sex is already over exploited? Pursuing the illusion promised by these books, many girls have naively and without full vision set themselves up for rapes, pregnancies and subsequent abortions. After reading such sexually explosive books, it is only natural for these unsuspecting teens of both sexes to wonder into the island of experimentation. Only few of them fully recover from the damage and scare. Some of the casualties become suitable candidates for the Porn Industry and other dangerous addictions in society after years of confusion and contradictions. But a far worse situation is that these unnecessary, and in fact, dangerous books could be allowed in our Public Schools but the Bible and other religious books are unconstitutional in Public Schools. Unbelievable!! Quoting statistics published in PARADE magazine of December 18, 1988, the author of THE MYTH OF SEPARATION said: "Two-thirds of America's 11 million teenage boys say they have had sex with a girl ...The first time for most of them was, when they were 15. By the time they were 18, on the average, boys have had sex with five girls." It would not be an exaggeration to double or triple that figure now. We decry teen school-drop-outs, teen pregnancies, excessive divorces and unstable families in society; but we are quiet about the so-called Planned Parenthood polluting the entire public school system of this country with destructive books as were mentioned above. They get our children at an early age, at the most vulnerable time of a teen's life. Do we need some binoculars to see the origin and connection of this society's madness? Do we need light to show us that something is definitely wrong in a judicial system, the political system and society, where it is unconstitutional for students to pray on school grounds but it is constitutional for teenagers to learn how to have sex? The truth of the matter is that neither teacher nor student is forcing or coercing anyone to join in prayer. But these books are part of the books officially allowed in the school. What happened to the "Congress shall make no law prohibiting the free exercise thereof;" of religion? In the school prayer situation, no one is establishing a religion "for all". So where is the violation? What part of the Constitution is infringed upon? If ACLU, Planned Parenthood and all the proponents of the so-called Separation of Church and State, say that religion has no place in the School; that religion belongs only in Churches and worship places, why do they not say that Sex and Sex Education belong with parents, in the bedroom and at home? If on the other hand sex education is a part of life, perhaps to teach young people responsible sexual behavior as the Creator meant it to be, why is religion not accorded, at least equal if not more recognition as a higher end than sex? Not only school prayer but different forms of religious expression should be taught in School. In no way can it be unconstitutional for students to prayer and acknowledge their Creator. Instead it is the "First Amendment" right of students to assemble to pray that has been violated by the Courts. It is difficult to understand that students' right to assemble as gangs, hazing groups, as cultists, as American Flag burners, and as gays and lesbians are protected; but they are not allowed to assemble to pray. As recently as 2006, a school district is allowing a class to be in the curricula "to desensitize" students from the use of profanity in school. Students will register for a class whose aim is to use, compete, teach, exchange and learn profanity. At the end of the semester the students will be examined and graded. Profanity can be a subject in school but God cannot be mentioned on school grounds. The Justices should think soberly about that and let their consciences be their judges. It is the future of minors we are talking about. It would be terribly immoral for the Justices to be contributing to the delinquency of minors by putting in place a national policy, a prohibition of something that would make these young people better citizens of the Nation. But it is clear that the absence of God in schools has had a devastating effect on our youths and society as a whole. The absence of Bibles, Qur'ans, and other sacred books of other religions, has spiritually bankrupted the American people in the long run. Children of America make up the America of tomorrow. The effect of the laws passed by Congress and judicial decisions of the Courts is evident in the number and intensity of crimes committed by students across America. The number of young men and women in the juvenile and prison systems, on account of indiscipline and criminal behavior, bear an excellent testimony to the absence of God in the school system. The number of violent and drug related crimes, among this segment of society, has been on a steady increase since the seventies. Children carrying guns and using them in schools, on streets, at home or in theatres, are quite familiar and *ordinary* in our society and those societies that have copied these policies from us. In the United States of America, there have been over a dozen student shootings in Public Schools since "The Columbine School Shootings". Yes indeed, it is often, ordinary and very casual, as if nothing has happened. It is no big deal for a youngster to take away the lives of innocent human beings without any remorse because the Courts through decisions and the society, through silence, and with a little help from ACLU and the like, have driven God out from the nucleus and center of learning – the family and the schools. If values are not taught or practiced in schools, how can society expect young people to exercise good moral judgment, which eventually will impact their behaviors from there on? Many of these young people spend a greater part of the day in school than with their parents and guardians, some of whom work two or three jobs. More than half of Americans don't go to Church, anyway. They are products of the same system. How are these young people supposed to get this godly and moral behavior that we expect of them? The fear and love of God are transmitted to people and are nourished by practice. If we have God in our school system, the fear and love of God would normally have demolished the present "culture of death", which was introduced to the country through Roe v. Wade, which, in turn has perpetuated the lack of sensitivity and reverence for human life, in our society and culture today.

FREEDOM AND THE AMERICAN FAMILY.

The family is the nucleus of society. It is society at its purest and its best. Many families make up what we call society. If the families of any society are good, that society will have to be good too. The converse is also true. The first family started with a man and a woman, Adam and Eve. The procreative power of God to Adam and Eve completes the family circle of father, mother with children. The family has its origin from God.

Freedom too originated from God through the free will He gave to Adam and Eve from the beginning. With it they could choose to do good or bad. Everyone therefore, who descended from Adam and

Eve, got this freedom to do right or wrong knowing the consequences of either.

When we look at the First Amendment of the Constitution, it is the same God-given right, which is being exercised. The goal is to treat everybody rightly and fairly in a group setting, which we call society. Anything done in the name of freedom, which is short of "justly" and "fairly", is no longer freedom. To activate ones free choice at the expense of other people's freedom, is nothing but selfishness. In relation to the First Amendment of the Constitution of America, freedom has been misread and misunderstood by a lot of people, including some Supreme Court Justices and members of Congress. In the case of the Justices, it is not lack of knowledge but a deliberate and purposeful agenda, which may be fuelled by selfishness or obedience to their *constituency*. This so-called misunderstanding of the First Amendment has adversely affected many aspects of American life. Its effects can be seen in the areas of *marriage, education, morality, responsible press,* and *law and order.* Practically all the present ills of American Society to date can be traced back to a misreading or misunderstanding of the First Amendment, which, by the way, is a good document. The First Amendment creditably served the Republic for close to two hundred years before it was assaulted and polluted and raped. But since the sixties, it is doubtful that the Founding Fathers themselves, if they were to pay us a visit, would even recognize the Amendments, which they put together, thanks to or no thanks to some of the Courts, some members of Congress, ACLU, and Feminist Groups' butchering of the Founding Fathers' intent.

The Courts have done a big 'number' on the family and Society through judicial activism. Unfortunately the Legislators have made some contributions along the same lines by constantly quoting, defending and endorsing Roe v. Wade, for an example, as *a settled law of the land.* Only a few short years ago, "Slavery" was also regarded as "a settled law and practice of the land" for many years. It was also "a settled law of the land" that blacks, in the United States of America, were until recently, not eligible to vote or be voted for. Women were not allowed to vote either. That too was a settled law of the land at one time. Should we have left them to continue to be "settled laws of the land"? Inter-racial marriages were aberrations, until recently. Abortion was illegal in these Republics until thirty three years ago. Before "Brown v. Board of Education", the separation of whites and blacks in public schools was upheld by the courts. That too was a settled law until something better came up – Brown v. Board of Education. In the same way, Roe v. Wade will be replaced by something better for America when America wakes up from her slumber. The time is coming. God is still running the show. Sometimes He lets us fool ourselves for a while.

The family has been broken down and love, which is the reason and foundation of the family, has been thrown out through the window because of what the Judges and politicians are doing in Washington DC and the fifty State capitals. Family discipline has been dismantled by the State and Federal Establishments. Parents are no longer running their families. The Social Welfare organ of the States has become the watchdog and surrogate parents. One could no longer advice, reprimand, or spank ones children without being hauled into jail and branded "child abuser". The only parents, who abuse their children, are those, whom the same system has messed up with drugs and promiscuity. The system gives them the license to fool around with sex, drinking and drugs and call it *Freedom*. The normal and average parent does not abuse his/her children. It is not the way God made it; it is not the way nature made it. The advocates of this policy of the State running the family for parents are the same people, who advocate that the Government has no business in the "privacy" of an individual or family. (Griswold v. Pennsylvania leading to Roe v. Wade) It is the same people, who do not want discipline in the homes or the schools that send their own children to private and religious schools. So, what is Government doing in our family living rooms if they want to defend "privacy" so badly? In school, small children, who do not know what child abuse is, are constantly asked stupid questions by teachers and counselors. They are advised to call the police if their parents spanked, or verbally reprimanded them. Sometimes children say yes to questions for the heck of it. "Abuse", physical and verbal have become household words. The Nation became a big advocate of children all of a sudden but still lets 1.3 million children to be killed every year through abortions.

What a balancing act - protecting children from their parents and aiding women and the same parents to slaughter their babies through abortions! What was the result?

Well, this mixed and double message made some women confused; some lost a sense and value of life. For some, life would never get its value back and that would scar them for life after abortions. This might lead to their hatred of children, men and life in general. But on the part of the children and the household, they would start running things and getting wild because they know where and when to press the button and someone in the house is hauled off to jail for days or weeks. Consequently parents became hostages in their own homes because they don't want to lose their children to the State or total strangers. In order to avoid jail time, parents would let the kids do whatever they want and whenever they want, as a kind of compromise to avoid constant visits from the police. When real love left the family, morality and God left too. A big crack at the family foundation obviously becomes a big crack in society itself. This family breakdown has a lot to do with the breakdown of society itself today. It becomes a vicious cycle. Naturally children and teens expect discipline and consequences for their actions from adults and family. When none is now forthcoming, they get a reinforcement to do the same or worse actions again and again. With that opening or crack in the family structure came indiscipline at home and in the classroom, under-age drinking, teen sex, drugs and alcohol addictions. This set of troubles does breed other sets of societal problems: grade school and high school drop-outs, stealing to maintain drug habits, violent homicide, illegitimate children, children having children, increased number of abortions, co-habitations, ill-prepared and sudden marriages and eventual divorces and remarriages, second, third, fourth, fifth and sixth times. The cycle begins all over again and is handed down from one generation to the other. One step leads to another and to another; it goes from one person to another, one family to another. We should not forget that all these behaviors started with Government misguided empowerment of children and the so-called war against abuse of children. When other Cultures and Countries, like India or some of our neighbors to the south, to mention just a few, try to teach their children to take care of themselves at a very early age, the

American government criticizes them for "abusing their children". At least in those cases, the children learn some good practical life experience. A lot of them put themselves through school and get to do the jobs our children could not do because they dropped out of school. The so-called "abused children" come here and compete with our children. They beat them in class and at work places.

The American Government seems to forget that the children she is replacing the parents with to "run" the household by her actions, are minors, who are not old enough to vote, drink alcohol, or drive a car; when they commit an offence, their names are withheld and they are tried in juvenile courts unless the crime is very vicious that they are tried in adults courts. If convicted, they are sent to a Juvenile Detention. After serving their sentence, their records are destroyed and they start life on a fresh page. Yet the Government emphasizes their so-called First Amendment Rights at the expense of the parents' Rights to raise their children. In actual fact, society is negatively empowering children by letting them get away without rules as well as consequences for bad choices. In a lot of ways it is like letting young people fend for themselves when everyone knows that they would fail. They receive mixed messages from their Leaders. Society tells them that they, as Americans, are free to do whatever they want. But when the free American children exercise this uninhibited freedom given to them by society, the same society locks them up in prisons for doing so. That is not fair to the children and not fair to the society that will ultimately put up with the misbehaviors of these misguided children.

EDUCATION:

When a teenager drops out from school, it is, in many cases, a sign of more serious problems ahead. Unless something profound happens, that particular teen would very likely find life more difficult than his or her counterpart who stayed in school. Both the teen drop-out and the family, in fact the society at large, would be worse for it. Every well-meaning person will agree that education lays the foundation for a person's future in more ways than one. When the prospects of that future are shattered by dropping out of school, the future becomes, at least uncertain but more often bleak. Some do, however, make it in life; but the number is very, very small in comparison. But since it is a human phenomenon for everybody to have needs, and many times we want things to survive, the individual teen would resort to unorthodox means of livelihood. Teen home and small store burglaries would probably be the first crimes in order to get by with a few essentials or maintain a drug habit. But sooner or later some door is going to open for the "big thing". The most lucrative of all is selling drugs. There is no suggestion here that only school drop-outs get involved in this "business". What is true is that the majority of people involved in it, do not have too much academic education. Invariably the teens, who sell drugs, do drugs too. For some the gain is what they use. They usually are in the middle or low end of the line. They would begin to make fast money as well as "get high" too. They would now be officially in the business of ruining their lives and those of other teenagers in the neighborhood, some of who will be partners and some customers. A very few drug dealers refrain from doing the "stuff" because they are smart enough to know that it is a dangerous tool that can destroy even the one handling it. These are the real Dealers, who make the real money out of it. If they began to mess with the drug itself, they would not be able to trace and control the money from the drug. This is a fast move on the part of the dealers; but this smart move reveals the intent of the dealers also namely to destroy lives while making money.

This is how a single mistake of dropping out of school could lead any teen to a dangerous path that could lead to his death or other people's deaths. Who would be responsible for his dropping out of school? Just read on. Apart from doing and selling drugs, this teen could also belong to a gang to protect his money, business and the empire. Even though he has a lot of money from the drug sale, he would need to have a sense of belonging, power and territorial conquest. With power, money and territory, come enemies as well as other problems. In most cases these young people have no family and no God. The gang members become their family and their "gods" would be money, luxury, power, drugs, sex and alcohol. With his gang family, these youngsters would terrorize the neighborhood with their "Homies". When they are in the mood and under the influence of these "gods" of theirs, then "what you see is what you get". The monster is let loose; life is reduced to nothing. Life is already nothing because abortions are constant happenings in their circles. After neighborhood operations, the streets are littered with the dead bodies of opposing gang members. But many times innocent bystanders become unfortunate victims of senseless killings, which the Police sometimes can do nothing about; and sometimes the Police become victims as well. After all, this is America, the land of "freedom" where anything goes in the "Hood". Is America ready to give back power to the parents to do their God-given job of raising their children?

FAMILY MORALITY AND EDUCATION:

There is interconnectedness in human affairs. As was said earlier, man is a whole entity that cannot be compartmentalized in a very real sense. Family, morality and education go hand in hand. So, who is to blame when a student drops out from school? Who is to blame when children grow to be a disappointment and an embarrassment to family and society? Who is to blame when young people become monsters and killing machines? Perhaps, there are enough blames to go round. It varies from one individual child, dropout or young adult to another child, dropout or young adult and from one environment to another. We are all culprits in this individually and collectively. First on that list would be parents, then School Boards, Governments – Local and State and sometimes the Church. Since we need the cooperation of all these and more, any lapse in one, some or all of these different essential organs, could drive a child off the edge. We cannot but repeat ourselves here because of the intertwined nature of man and human affairs. Parents, governments and churches need to work together as collaborators to bring up the next generation of Americans.

A teenager's future could be derailed by an irresponsible Dad, who is not at home, a Dad, who is a sponge; he could be set off by a Dad, who has no religious values or some higher being to be accountable to for his life, actions and responsibilities. If one denies the necessity of "religious values" in an individual, there might not be any need to live, be a good person, not to inflict pain on other people, or stay home with family and raise his children and take good care of his wife. What would be the incentive to stop drinking or doing drugs if there is no God or Life after death? Many of the men and women in prison had no Dads in the house, had at least one of the parents drinking or doing drugs, did not or rarely went to Church. If one does not believe in life after death, what is the use of life or raising children to become good citizens? Who needs children anyway, when one can have sex any time and abort babies if there happens to be an accidental pregnancy? If this is the Dad's philosophy, what would be the use of education for his kids? The welfare of his children would not be part of his immediate concern. Getting high on anything would be more of a concern for him than taking care of his children. For a child, who knows that his father is a drunkard, or even realizes that his Dad is often never home and when he is home is drunk or beating his Mom, there is no future or interest to study or do home-work or even in getting married or having children of his own. For a child whose Dad, has never thought him any values, never took him to a ball game, play basket ball, fishing or to worship some form of Deity, there is little or no hope for him to be somebody, go to school or take the trouble of being disciplined. What for? When there is no man in the house to help the woman in raising the children, the children have a very narrow chance of making it in the world. They grow fast too quickly. Very few have made it; even then it is an uphill task.

Different levels of government in this country have, through legislations, created the environment that has been hostile to the family (man, woman and child) to be happy together. Nature designed that it takes a man and a woman to have children; so it takes a man and a woman to raise them too. Without prejudice to some exceptions, single-motherhood in America has unfortunately been "beatified". It is almost raised and praised to a point of a Nobel Prize category especially during political campaigns. That is regrettably one of the causes of the fractures we see in the American family of today. The single-motherhood phenomenon is a child of the seventies, eighties, the nineties and is still waxing strong. Many of the parents, of course are the products of the sixties. The beatification is exacerbated by attendant family problems like divorce, teen pregnancies and unwed moms all of which caused a "bad rap" for genuine single moms like widows. Apart from widows, single-motherhood was an exception before the sixties. But now the single life-style is becoming very attractive to young ladies because Holly-Wood has given it a boost and added prominence. If a woman has money, what does she need a man for when she can get one or many on her bed anytime she wants? What does a rich lady need a husband for when she can tailor her own baby with whomsoever she wants? Some married women Company Executives have found single-motherhood attractive. So why keep a man in the house? Fire him. Who is running things around here? She is; though he thinks he is. When there is a divorce which of the spouses gets the house? She does. If the property is divided fifty, fifty, she still gets alimony unless he has a good Attorney and goes after her money aggressively. You can't beat that. Who needs a man? Somebody made that attractive deal. There are a few "playboys" in that kind of life style. Who suffers the crash in-spite of all that money? The children do!

Two rich men or two women can opt to live together as domestic partners with adopted children. This kills the whole notion of family and marriage. Not everything we can physically do is good for us or society. Because we have the freedom and the means to do something does not make it right. This society is not going to fulfill its goal and mission assigned her by God until the different governments give back appropriate roles to children, parents and the Church.

A teen could quit school because her Mom is a drug addict (junkie) and or an alcoholic. She sees her life as useless because nobody gives her any attention she deserves; nobody appreciates the work she does at school; nobody comes to her games because her Mom is under the influence (drunk or high) most of the time and she does not know where or who her Dad is. There is no peace of mind when she comes home from school because the house is full of foul language and cursing or the parents are fighting if the Dad is in the house or with the Mom's boy-friend when her Dad has moved out. In a divorce situation, it is sad enough for her that her Mom has a live-in junkie boy-friend; they cannot stop quarreling and fighting. Sleeping on the streets, being picked up by a stranger, moving in with a man, or joining a "gang" family would be better than staying at home in that environment. There goes the classroom. She could become a dropout. Invariably this innocent, teenage student could become an alcoholic or drug addict or unwed Mom, with a number of abortions and perhaps, a criminal in juvenile or adult prison. It must be noted that one *rarely* gets involved with *just* one of these addictions and problems; they always go together because the individuals involved have no foundation in values or authentic religion. These vices are comfortable with each other. These destructive qualities have a common enemy in God, moral values and decency.

Before teenagers "go off the hook", they show warning signs of trouble. Early signs of depression and total disappointment in life show forth. They begin to avoid family gatherings. They skip meals, come home late and are generally withdrawn. Many times the parents don't see these signs because they are too busy with work or business or they are concentrating on themselves with boy-friends/girl-friends and the troubles they created in their own relationships. Divorce of parents is the most devastating thing to a child or a teenager. In a single and apparently simple act of divorce, children lose all sense of parental protection and the feeling of emptiness takes over. This state of affairs is manifested in the child or teenager acting up and acting out. There is a manifestation of unruliness, deviant behaviors in talking, acting and dressing. External appearance means nothing to them at this point. They don't care for or about anything or anybody. The more bizarre their appearance, the better for their psyche! Eye, nose, tongue, and lips piercing and body tattoos are one of the first manifestations of real troubles. Posing nude for a magazine would be a consideration at some point. Very good teenagers could all of a sudden, flip out like that and become problem children because adults in their lives could not control their selfishness in the face of temptation and marital problems.

Marriage And Divorce:

Many, many marriages before the sixties were happy and lasting relationships. Most people then knew what marriage was: a holy union of a man and a woman to raise their children in the love and fear of God; it was a union of love, understanding and support one for another, a union of a couple, which truly understood that marriage should go on for better, for worse, in sickness and in health, in good times and in bad; it used to be a union where the welfare of the children came before the parent's ego and selfish interests. Life was simple and good because, in most homes, God was part of the events of each household. Children were raised with moral values; they were taught right and wrong and how to do the right thing and avoid the wrong thing. This was passed on from one generation to another. The family was not run by the government. Divorce was extremely rare. But it was not rare to see numerous couples celebrate fifty, sixties years of happy married life with many children, grand and great grand children. The children turn out good even though the income then was small. In most cases only one spouse brought home a pay-check. But everybody was happy. So, what exactly went wrong? Where did we drop the ball?

There were so many factors that contributed to the moral decay that caused the American family to disintegrate. As has already been stated, the violence on the family was consciously or unconsciously put in place after the two world wars, but it matured in the sixties with the powerful force of *women liberation*, which ushered in the sexual revolution of the sixties. That was the first blow to the stable, happy and integrated family system. We are seeing the last of that age group in their senior years now. Their children are fairly doing fine. But after that, it has been very, very tough to keep the family together anymore. That is why fifty per cent of American marriages end up in divorce now. If you add to that mix, the number of people living together without marriage, the single and unmarried women with children, the magnitude of the moral decadence in society today will begin to surface and perhaps be better understood as a national disaster. Too many Americans marry too young and a great many of them exhibit a cavalier attitude to marriage. For many couples, it was just a casual thing one does at a certain age. From the onset many such marriages are destined to go nowhere any way. Does it surprise any one what happens when a man picks up a girl in a Bar and supposedly "falls in love" with her and gets married in Reno or on the Beach or in the air jumping out from a plane with a self-proclaimed minister friend of one of the couple? What a place to pick a life partner. A Bar! Who is surprised when there is an "irreconcilable difference" a few miles down the road?

One of the big players is again the Government. The Local, State and Federal governments, have the power to arm and disarm people. And these governments have done both in this case. They have empowered people to do bad things and have effectively disarmed parents, for instance, by incapacitating parents from managing their families. There is a wrong assumption by Government that she can raise children better than parents. It is only in a few extreme cases that parents should be restricted from active participation in the raising of their children. These are purely parents who are drug addicts or have mental disabilities or have sexual deviant behaviors. Even such parents are products of the same system in question. Incompetent parents are new in this society. We did not see many such parents before the sixties. The present mal-adjusted parents are a result of the new liberation movement, which created alcohol and drug addicted mothers. The Government should only get closely involved with such families, which need help to kick off the habit. With regard to other families, the Government should only be by the side encouraging parents in raising their children. Government should fund the children's education in public and private schools and let parents choose which schools their children go to, public or private, provided the private schools are accredited by Government. Children should not be discriminated against because they choose to go to private schools, where there is no violence or drug use. After all children in private schools are American children too. Their parents, grand parents, aunts and uncles pay taxes too. In fact good behavior in private schools should be an incentive to Government to clean up the public schools and find out what makes these private schools tick. What makes private schools great is that the maintenance of discipline is the first order of business. Students obey and respect the teachers; that disposes and relaxes the teachers to love their students and teach well. There is a certain degree of decorum necessary for learning. People do not learn in a war zone or in fear. Little or no learning goes on in an atmosphere and environment infested with gangs, fashion parade and explicit immoral behaviors.

In private schools, every student wears some form of simple and clean uniform. With the uniform system and parents becoming helpers not obstructionists in the school, private schools and families become effective partners in the education of the children. The parents of every student in the public school should sign an agreement that they would not interfere with the day to day running of their children's school. Instead of backing their wards when they act up in school, parents should re-enforce the punishment given by the school authorities. The existence of uniforms will eliminate the baggy and over size clothes that facilitate the smuggling of weapons and drugs into the school. Added to that fact is that there would not be any more unnecessary distractions and competition of clothes and fashion in schools by rich and poor students. The girls would not be showing the whole world their belly buttons for a change. Boys would concentrate more on their school work and less about pulling up their pants every two minutes because the pants are slipping and falling off their waist. By maintaining the dress code, the school would make sure that a student, whose waist is 34 inches, gets a 34 inch waist pants and not 44 or 54 inches. Will the Government help to do that? Will the politicians have the courage to enforce that in the public school system? No, because it is not politically correct. ACLU will not go along with it either. This is part of the problems that the youths face. Let it be on record that young people are not bad people. We make them so. Standard school uniform is one big and sure way of cutting down on the number of student drop out, violence and drugs in the nation's school system. Private schools have shown that it works. Does the Electorate have the courage to put this in place? Once again, the answer is no! Instead those who can afford it will prefer to pay to send their children to private schools to sending them to a free public school infested with violence and drugs, which are good ingredients for low grades and failure. What does that tell us about people in Government paying big bucks to send their own children to private schools and they are running fee-free and failed public schools? One of the so-called "freedom advocates", the ACLU will come up with reasons against uniforms in schools, that it will violate the students' First Amendment right to wear whatever they want to wear. These are kids, who cannot vote or drive. What if some students want to go to school naked everyday as a part of their rights under the Constitution as freedom of expression? What will ACLU say then? This goes to show that a lot of people, including ACLU, have no idea what FREEDOM means; they have no idea the scope and limits of freedom and they are supposed to be educated people. One cannot but ask some questions: Does the idea of Freedom suggest that people in uniforms are less free? Why do our Generals, Admirals, and other officer ranks in the Armed forces wear the uniform and the ACLU has said nothing? Thousands of Police Officers, Catholic school students, Firefighters and Coast Guards proudly wear their uniforms everyday. ACLU does not call it degrading. How about Boys and Girl Scouts of America? Commercial Pilots, Air Hosts and Hostesses majestically show up for work everyday at the Airports in uniforms. Is freedom here to serve us or are we here to serve freedom? There are hundreds of other groups that wear and are proud of their uniforms everyday in this country and ACLU does not think it is infra-dig to wear uniforms in those circumstances. Why does ACLU think that Grade and High school students should be treated differently on the issue of school uniform? It can only mean that there is an ulterior motive, which is not good for society. Somebody must have an agenda to misdirect young children. Somebody is having fun with students' shooting in school.

Why do people of the world embrace freedom? Is it just for freedom's sake or is it to help people to grow, improve and forge ahead with a view to becoming good and productive citizens? What happens when the exercise of one or some people's freedom does harm or sets us back or makes us kill ourselves or ushers in violence or chaos in society? Do we still exercise that kind of freedom because the Constitution calls for us to be free? What are we being free from? Which of this nonsense libertarian attitude is ignorance; which is patronizing and which is pure malice? The American Civil Liberties Union are mainly lawyers; they could not be ignorant in those areas they get involved in. If we know what works and some people don't let it happen, it should make it clear that some people are taking pleasure in young Americans dying daily of drug overdose, sleeping in gutters and stealing to support drug habits, dropping out of school, shooting one another as gang members, prostituting to buy drugs, getting involved in under age sex and drinking in the name of Freedom.

After seeing the score-board, do we still want to give ACLU the benefit of the doubt?

The casual way in which, people get married these days, is even getting more alarming. A man would meet a woman in a bar and a week later they are married in Reno or Las Vegas, Nevada or jumping off the plane saying "I do". A few months or years down the line, they are divorced on account of 'irreconcilable differences'. Government is not helping the situation either. It is the governments and the courts, which designed these shallow relationships that are based on emotion or rather 'nothing' but feeling. I love the naïve reason that is given for the dissolution of marriages in the courts: "irreconcilable difference". How would you feel if God used the same line on you when you come to reconcile with him? It baffles the mind that the couple, who yesterday were "'Honey, Honey', 'Sweetheart, Sweetheart', 'Baby, Baby', 'Sugar, Sugar' and 'I can't live without you', will come out a few years after and talk about irreconcilable difference. It is even more baffling when these same couples go through the same emotions of "falling in love", "marriage", "falling out of love" and then "divorce", "remarry" three, four up to seven times. It speaks a lot not only about their concept of marriage but of their total disregard for the children born of these so-called marriages. It reflects on the society that feeds and condones the practice. For one thing a lot of people, who get married, have no idea what marriage is about. Embedded in that is the fact that they don't know what love is. They could never have been in love in the first place. When people say they are in love, they should realize that love is about giving and not about the Ego at the receiving end; they should know that love is God.

Here the Churches have also failed the people woefully as the Government has by not preparing them well to know what it is they are going into; that in their marital union they are encountering a person, the Second Person of the Trinity. That person, Jesus Christ, is the glue that keeps the marriage together and strong, if the union was established in Him. If couples understood that love is about forgiving, they would not be talking about irreconcilable differences. If couples knew that love is about exercising patience and endurance for the beloved, if they knew that it is about being kind to "Sweetheart" or "Honey" at all times in spite of his or her failures, if they knew that it is not about registering the wrongs of each other or brooding over one another's injuries and mistakes, there would be scarcely any divorces taking place. If couples knew that love is about putting their children first, no couple would file for a divorce. So a lot of couples are ignorant of what they enter into when they say "I do" and the Church gets some of the blame. Couples don't know what they are doing in marriage. They mistake infatuation for love. What they feel and commit to is external beauty, money and or accomplishments, not internal grace and beauty, which are spiritual realities only seen by the wise. When the exterior deteriorates, as it must, the so-called love evaporates. As some people say, "they fall out of love". That is the evidence that they do not know that love is eternal. It does not die and cannot fade. One cannot fall "out of it" either. It is eternal; it is Christ. It is God. Who shares a big chunk of the blame? The Churches do; the religious leaders, the priests and pastors do. The priests have sub-let the job of individually preparing and counseling couples, who are preparing to get married, to franchises like "Pre-Cana" or "Engaged week-end" or some other names. There is nothing wrong with these groups. In fact they are a necessary component to the over all preparation of couples before marriage. But a one day seminar or one weekend should not take the place of the priest's pastoral education of couples before they say "I do". One of the reasons why there is a regulation for couples tell the priest the date of their wedding six months ahead of time is for the priest to have enough time for series of meetings with the couple before the wedding. The need to do this is exacerbated by the fact that over fifty percent of the engaged couples do not have enough knowledge of the teachings of the Church especially on the Sacraments; some are involved in mixed marriages, which constitute their own unique problems. The experience is that in mixed marriages, many couples do not practice anything afterwards. One couple will stop his or her religious practice in deference to the other spouse. In some cases the children do not have any religion or at least, don't practice anything either. If priests and pastors were to take this duty seriously, the rate of divorce in this country would be cut down drastically.

One other contributor to divorce is "dating". Dating could be likened to the First Amendment, which has over the years been misunderstood and misread. The idea of dating by itself is good. But like the First Amendment, it has been overstretched to a point of infamy and ridicule. In America, people can do almost anything, link it to the First Amendment and get away with it. The same thing is applicable to dating. Dating, as it is now, is a joke, which encourages fornication and adultery and constitutes a recipe for divorce. Originally dating was a way of finding a suitable life partner in marriage. A prospective dating couple would go out from time to time to study each other to see if they were compatible for marriage. The goal was always to get married. After a number of months or years of "dating", if there is a real "spark" in the relationship, the two would get engaged. Sometimes it is announced through the media. But family members will know even if it is not publicly announced. This stage of the game is still an elevated form of dating. It may take three or six months or even a year after the engagement before the couple will get married, if they still see the good qualities in each other. There is no sexual activity in this relationship at this time. Their focus at this stage is the "faith" concerns and the matching of minds and personalities. The best is saved for the last, as they say. Faith compatibility was a big part of this period. One would like to live with one who has the same belief system as the partner. That was then; this is now.

While dating was primarily a preparation for marriage, now it is primarily for fun. People, who have no intention of getting married, go out on dates. It is so casual that some date every week with different partners. Kids in elementary schools have girl friends and boy friends and they go out. Everybody seems to encourage this. This is one of the so many bad teachings of our behavioral scientists, who think it is a good thing. Psychologists and psychotherapists teach that it is a necessarily good practice. Some even go so far as to suggest that if teen boys and girls don't date there would be an increase in the number of gays we have. What a theory! There are more gays now than any time in the American history. In fact those countries, which do not date as Americans, have little or no gays. Many people may get fade up with the early introduction to dating that they would be willing to try gay life style for a change.

The jury has been back and the verdict has not been good. The jury tells us that one out of every two marriages ends in a divorce. Yet the practice continues. Another verdict is that there are more sexually transmitted diseases now than then. There are more depression, teen suicide, drug use and date rapes and date-drug rapes among teens now than then. What is a grade school student, whose preoccupation should be his/her studies, doing with a date? Is it for more distractions because there are enough in their lives already? That and more! The custom of Elementary and High School students dating adversely affects their education, causes premature sexual activity and sexually transmitted diseases, teen pregnancy leading to more abortions and ultimately divorce, down the road, if and when they eventually marry. The modern dating happens to be the greatest contributor to abortion and divorce in the United States of America and else where. This is how it happens. Among teens, young adults and some adults, dating is primarily for fun. There is nothing serious about the relationship. If anything is happening, it is a way, an easy way of getting a sex partner and "having fun". There is no love attached to it since none has any idea what love is. It is all physical infatuation. Consequently in a given year one could have ten, twenty and up to thirty girl or boy friends for dates. Do the mathematics over a period of ten to twenty years. How many partners has one person averaged in dating and sex and hopping from one partner to another? There you go. That is a lot of on and off switching of emotions by one individual to be emotionally stable for a permanent relationship in marriage later. Emotional instability is very hard to fix. Such situations predispose divorce subsequently. Again, since it is physical, there is a lot of ego and experimentation involved and feelings are easily hurt. It is a relationship built on "feelings" not love or trust. It is a relationship, which is easy to come by and such relations are terminated easily because they don't have any foundation in something concrete or spiritual. Over time those teens or young adults and adults unconsciously develop a certain inability to make and keep a good relationship built on mutual respect with the opposite sex because all the relationship they had known so far and for so long was jump from one relationship to another. They become addicted to not staying in a relationship for long. There again we have divorce written all over it. They could not remember how many times they had given a similar or the same answer to this question:

"How is Jack?" or

"How is Mary?" Answer: "We broke up."

"We are no longer seeing each other."

They had broken up so many times in the dating years that it has become second nature for them to start a relationship and break up. It is easier to be dating perpetually than to have one partner all the time, children and responsibility to take care of. This is what dating has done to so many Americans. The Nigerian culture does not take kindly to that kind of attitude. Hence Nigeria does not date the way America dates. For the dating boy in America, girls are things one uses for fun; he can dump them and pick up some more. For the girl, boys are things she spins around her finger, uses them for fun and dumps them for any reason at all or wait until there is "a new kid on the block" to check out.

When eventually they settle down, to get married and have children, they discover that they get irritated over any small thing. It is not them; it is a condition. Unless they work at it, it is impossible to stay in a relationship which is by definition a give and take relation. Dating did not train them to give of themselves; it did not train them to be selfless. So they can stay. They do what they have always done – cut and run, break-up to find another. And life goes on. While honestly some of them are doing their best to live a good married life; they cannot get over the idea of fun and dating; the "take and pass-on" mentality is subconsciously still very much alive. Depending on the individuals concerned, one in two will end in a divorce. For a lot of them it is agonizing to go through the process of give and take, forgive and be forgiven, which are part of marriage. Nobody prepared them for the ordeal, which is more than just having "fun". A number of them will not know what hit them until it is too late. They, to a certain extent, become victims of the system and the society, which made them to behave the way they do. But the children of these marriages are the real victims, who in a few short years would fall through the same cracks and commit a worse assault on marriage and the family. And the cycle continues. But it is time to break the cycle and rescue the family for the good of all. Since Government is supposed to be for the people's good, she should step up to the plate and play her role to protect the people and make them happy in the real sense of the word. Otherwise the fifty percent divorce rate will hit seventy five percent in the next generation. Politicians, where is "The Government of the people by the people for the people"?

3. Freedom of speech and press:

In Europe, before the birth of the United States of America, religious persecution was common. There was persecution when one expressed religious opinions that were contrary to those of the king or ruler of the land. The press was not free to write against the king or queen. Since the people did not choose their kings or queens, they had no right to express opinions if the rulers were not doing justice to the people. If they did express some dissatisfaction, they were persecuted or even killed. Even as British subjects in the Colonies, the first American immigrants could not criticize the British Government or voice their opinion even in the colonies and on American soil without persecution. To live in that kind of intimidation and fear in the new land was not an option for the Founding Fathers after their hard-fought Freedom. Hence the Freedom of Speech and Press Clause was something they had to put down in writing in order to avoid the same situation they ran away from in Europe as well as the situation they experienced in the Colonies under British rule. This is the historical context of the Freedom of Speech and Press Clause of the First Amendment. The Founding Fathers wanted the "small man's" voice to be heard. They did not want the government to use her weight and power to clamp down on the people of the United States neither did they want individuals to undermine the efforts of Government.

But unfortunately the Courts and the ACLU and the like have put a new spin and meaning on the freedom of speech and press clause of the First Amendment. For them Freedom now means to do or say practically anything under the sun. Of late decency laws do no longer exist because the Courts treat all speeches, irrespective of content, as protected under the Free Speech Clause of the First Amendment of the Constitution. This unconstitutional protection itself creates lawlessness in society. People can no longer be charged with crimes if they openly call for violence on a person or group of persons like the police officers or elected officials, who have differing opinions. People could openly call for violence or terrorism and pass for free speech. This is very true of a number of rappers and Activists, who preach hatred across the Nation. In a 1973 case, (Miller v. California) Chief Justice Burger, writing for the majority opinion in an obscenity case, defined the First Amendment thus: it "protects works which, taken as a whole have serious literary, artistic, political, or scientific value, regardless of whether the government or majority of people approve of the ideas these works represent." What, perhaps, could be the literary, artistic, political, and scientific value of cursing, encouraging suicide, illicit sex, alcohol and drugs in a rap or song or writing or protest? Is denigrating women an art form? Is encouraging criminals to kill Cops an expression of art or a form of science? It must be pointed out here that the youth are the largest consumers of 'rap' in this country and perhaps many other countries. In other words, these young people, the most delicate in our society, are being encouraged to commit suicide, shoot and kill anyone, drink alcohol, engage in sexual activity before marriage and use illegal drugs and denigrate our women and burn the American Flag openly. The Constitution would be encouraging the killing of Cops and who knows who or what group will be next – members of Congress or Justices. May be somebody will then wake up to see that, that was not what the Founding Fathers meant by free speech and free press. But thank God that is not what the First Amendment meant by freedom of speech. And it is a protected action/speech to teach how to make bombs and other explosives and devices on the internet. What good is that to society? It is free speech and free expression to burn the American Flag, which is the symbol of the Nation. The proponents of Flag Burning would argue that it is a way of protest, a way to seek redress. Let us for a moment take that as a valid reason to burn the American Flag. What happens when another individual burns the City Council Building in protest for whatever he thinks the County did or did not do? Shall we let it go unpunished because he/she was exercising his/her First Amendment free expression and right --eh? What will happen if one race or group marches up to the Hill in thousands and sets some of the Congressional buildings ablaze in protest because

Congress passed a law that this group thinks is unjust? Will there be no arrests for arson? Do we sincerely want to believe that burning the American Flag by Americans was what the Founding Fathers meant by **freedom of speech?** I doubt it. Think for a moment. Why do protesters from other nations burn the American Flag for when they are angry with American policies regarding their country? They want to denigrate America, of course. They want to hurt America from any distance they are. Another food for thought: Why is it that the <u>Legislators and Judges,</u> who were closer in proximity to the Founding Fathers, did not interpret the freedom of speech clause as we do now, more than two hundred years later? And behold, we claim to be interpreting the intentions of the Founding Fathers, more than two hundred years removed from the Framers. What were the then Legislators and Judges doing, would you say? <u>Misinterpreting the Constitution, would you say?</u> Are the interpretations of the earlier Judges not closer to the intentions of the Framers of the Constitution than those of the recent Judges, since the earlier Judges lived closer to the Framers of the constitution? It is clear to any well meaning person that the Founding Fathers of the Constitution understood that "freedom" without "limitation" is nothing but slavery, slavery to human instincts and impulses. Freedom without some limit or inhibition is but anarchy and lawlessness, namely to do or say whatever one likes, whenever one likes, to whomever one wants with impunity. But as human beings, we are called to higher things than just being the slaves of passions, feelings and instincts. There is a big difference between us and the big old crocodiles or other wild animals, which are ready to instinctively pounce on anyone within their proximity. Humans think before they act, unlike the croc which does not think, as humans do. There are no moral consequences to animals' actions.

There is a certain degree of inequity and hypocrisy in the defense of unwholesome behaviors and speeches. If a person talks or dresses or 'raps' indecently; burns the American Flag, that individual would be defended and protected under the First Amendment's freedom of speech clause. What do you suppose would happen if another person exercises the same freedom of speech clause by denigrating or rapping about the gays and lesbians, the black people, the Koreans or

Vietnamese people in America? All hell would break loose. It would be declared unconstitutional by the same advocates of free speech and expression. Is this inequity and hypocrisy or what? It is almost like eating your cake and still have it or wanting to be a great surgeon but can't stand the sight of blood or wanting to be pilot but you are afraid of heights. It does not work like that and does not make sense either. Could we apply the same rules to a group of school children exercising their freedom of expression by assembling on the school ground and worship their God? Of course not! Freedom of speech does not always apply when one is doing something good. It is okay when one is cursing out a politician or the President, dancing naked on the street or demonstrating, burning the national flag, making fun of Jesus Christ hanging on the Cross, making fun of the Nuns' uniform in a gay parade or may be teaching people how to make bombs on the internet to blow up people. Those would enjoy the status of freedom of speech. What a freedom of speech, hypocrites!

The Supreme Court made a free expression decision recently that seems to contradict itself. It is the display of the Ten Commandments' cases. On the last day of the Supreme Court's 2004-2005 Session, the highest Court in the land ruled that the six foot granite marker of the Ten Commandments could be displayed on the grounds of Texas Statehouse, while calling for the removal of the Ten Commandments displayed in two Kentucky Court Houses. In a 5-4 decision, the Justices ruled that the Texas Ten Commandments display is constitutional because it is one of a number of secular displays. In other words some of the five Justices saw it as a secular display and not a religious one. Justice Stephen Breyer, who cast the decisive vote in the two cases, said that the fact that the Texas monument has been there for 40 years before there was a suit to remove it means it was not likely to be divisive. (How many years was abortion illegal in the United States before it was challenged and overturned in 1973, one might ask?) On the Texas case, the Chief Justice William Rehnquist said that the court had never barred "any and all government preference for religion over irreligion". He cited the 1983 ruling allowing prayers by chaplains at legislative sessions and the May, 2005's ruling upholding a federal law that protects prisoners' religious practices. The Chief Justice and those on his side in this case made a very crucial distinction, which some people don't seem to acknowledge, namely that the government is entitled to favor religion, as long as it uses no coercion and shows no preference for a particular religion. That seems to be what the Framers would say if they were here today. The government is supposed to encourage people to be religious. At least that is one way of having orderliness, tolerance, peace and quiet in society. These are all part of the Ten Commandments. I think that Chief Justice Rehnquist put it best when he said that government had not in the past favored irreligion. But today we have the signs of irreligion all over in our public schools and elsewhere. There is an outright "hostility" against religion. Every fair minded person will agree that people who were properly raised in religion behave better in society than those who were not. They are more peaceful and loving than people who were raised with no religion. There is no morality, no standard, no justice and no sense of equity in people, who have no sense of religion or the sacred. The chance of a Columbine school type shooting rampage happening in a private Religious School environment, would be one in a million schools. I will deal with this a little more in depth later. One might say: if government encourages religion, it might bring about people wanting government to recognize any bizarre practice in the name of religion. To begin with, there are some characteristics of religion that everybody on any side of the issue will agree with. It will have to look religion, smell religion, taste religion and act religion to enjoy the favors of State. Yes, that fear might exist; and that is part of what is happening now and what is wrong with the way we are interpreting "freedom" in this country. It would be absurd, for instance, to allow a group of people, who engage in human sacrifice, to enjoy the status of religion. The government would not let that happen, of course.

In another 5-4 ruling, the Court ruled that the two Ten Commandments cases in Kentucky were unconstitutional because the two displays were put there on religious grounds. This is splitting hair. What if a person tells the truth in court for religious reasons! Moreover the majority opinion stated that other secular artifacts were placed there after the law suit had been filed. In his dissent on the two Kentucky cases, Justice Antonin Scalia accused the majority opinion of *hostility* to religion and ignorance of history and tradition of

America. He continued: "The Ten Commandments are a foundation of the rule of law, and a symbol of the role that religion played, and continues to play, in our system of government." This is a piece of history that cannot be ignored. This Nation was founded on religion and is accommodative of all religions. It would be unfair to the Founding Fathers for the present courts to be hostile to religion, as is the case now. The only thing the Founding fathers did not want was "coercion" and or "preference" of one religion over another. To place reminders like the Ten Commandments and Crosses at strategic places for those who care to look at them is a healthy thing for society. Like any other poster on the highway, no one is forced to look at it. It would have been unconstitutional if the Ten Commandments were allowed to be displayed and the Hindus or Moslems' equivalent of the Ten Commandments, were refused to be displayed if they wanted a display of their own. Not letting religious symbols in public places is tantamount to discrimination and hostility toward religion. And that is in itself, unconstitutional; "free exercise thereof" is ignored. But Justice Scalia could not have said it better that the majority opinion in those two Kentucky Ten Commandment cases have forgotten the religious history of this Nation. In our courts, people put their right hand on the Bible as they take oaths, and Presidents still put their right hands on the Bible when they take the oath of office. That means that every court in the land has a copy of the Bible in place ready for use before a witness testifies. And where did the Ten Commandments come from? The Bible, of course! Is it an endorsement of religion for the Federal Government to have a copy of the Bible in courts or to recruit and pay Military Chaplains? Is it unconstitutional for Counties and State Governments to hire the services of Chaplains in jails and prisons and pay them with the people's money? Where do the Supreme Court Judges on the left get this stuff? This is a dangerous trend.

For all intents and purposes, the Supreme Court seemed to have confused both the people and the lower courts when she ruled that the Ten Commandments can stay in Texas Statehouse but cannot in the two cases of Kentucky. "How is a government official to know whether some particular practice is OK?" asked UCLA law professor, Eugene Volokh. He thinks that Justice Breyer used a test whose outcome is virtually unpredictable. How does one know that a certain display endorsed religion and a similar display does not? (As if the practice of religion is a crime to be eradicated) The issue here seems to be whether the public display expresses a government alliance with religion or simply an acknowledgement of a religious heritage of the nation and its laws. It will be impossible for government not to have a general alliance with religion because it is dealing with people of religion and religion has a role to play in government. The radical reason and truth of this assertion is because man is a religious, thinking animal, which has intellect and will to know and worship a Supreme Being. Man happens also to be the one representing man in the government of man. The only time there will be a problem with the Constitution is when government has a preference to one particular religion and forces everyone to that religion at the exclusion of others. It would be unconstitutional if government refuses to let a religious group display their religious artifacts on government property where another religious group did display one. As Justice Scalia pointed out, the courts should not be "hostile" to religion at all. Without the Ten Commandments and other ancient religious laws, we would not have a justice system as we have today, in the first place. The Elder Statesmen of the Republic knew the importance of the Ten Commandments. The United States Supreme Court Building has some of the world's law-givers with Moses prominently displaying the Ten Commandments. As one enters the Supreme Court courtroom, the two huge oak doors have the Ten Commandments engraved on the lower portion of each door. On the wall right above where the Justices sit, there is a display of the Ten Commandments there. Therefore our laws and the adjudication of them have a very close tie with the Ten Commandments and the Justice System. Do the Supreme Court Justices, who alienate God from the Courts, realize that there are biblical verses etched in stone all over the Federal buildings and Monuments in Washington D. C.? I would be insulting them if I said they didn't. James Madison, the 4th President of the United States of America, also known as "The Father of the Constitution" said:

"We have staked the whole of all our political institutions upon the capacity of mankind for self-government, upon the capacity of each and all of us to govern ourselves, to control ourselves, to sustain ourselves according to the Ten Commandments of God."

What is it in the Ten Commandments that is odious to some people? As President Madison said, it is the Ten Commandments that help us all to love and respect God and one another.

Since 1777 every session of Congress has begun with a prayer said by a Chaplain. All United States Presidents have ended their oath of office with: "So help me God." Who knows what the next Supreme Court will say about that? There are already law suits challenging "In God we trust" on our money as well as "under God" in the pledge of allegiance. Just last week, a Judge in San Francisco ruled for a Sacramento man, who wanted "One Nation under God" removed from the Pledge. It was not the intention of the Founders of this Nation to have a Godless society as some people want to make us believe today. These people happen to be in the minority; yet they have loud voices and are very persistent. America has a history here to protect. Some liberal judges have been trying to unbalance and change our history. It is about time that people on the other side wake up and become a little more aggressive than they currently are. It is not accidental that God featured in some places like 'the pledge of allegiance', 'our money' in 'the oath of office' and 'the national anthem'. The third verse of the anthem reads:

"O thus be it ever when freemen shall stand
Between their lov'd homes and the war's destination!
Blest with vict'ry and peace, may the heavens-rescued land
Praise the Pow'r that hath made and preserved
Us a nation!
Then conquer we must, when our cause it is just!
And this be our motto: "In God is our trust!"
And the Star-Spangled Banner in triumph shall wave
O'er the land of the free and the home of the brave!

The question is: Why are these people so anti God and anti Religion? There are a lot of Ten Commandments cases now in the works. There is one filed by a Pleasanton, California lawyer regarding the Ten Commandments on the official seal of the 9th U.S. Circuit

Court of Appeals in San Francisco. We may wake up one morning and hear that the doors to the Supreme Court are torn down. With regard to the case in California we may wake up one morning and hear that the Ten Commandments on the official seal of the 9th U. S. Circuit Court of Appeals and the ceiling tile in one of its Courtrooms, are all torn down because, after all these years, they have become unconstitutional. When will this madness stop? Where do we draw the line that enough is enough? That is what happens when freedom is made to mean welcoming the absurd.

When are we as a Nation going to tell ACLU and the National Organization for women to back off? The Supreme Court, and indeed, the nation is becoming a laughing stock because of their positions on "School Prayer", "The National Flag burning", "Under God" in the Pledge of Allegiance, and "Cross burning" by hateful people, to just mention some. In America, under the First Amendment, Ku Klux Klan can burn the Holy Cross on someone's lawn or in a public square. But could anyone dare do it to a Moslem emblem? Try it as a free expression and see. How would you decide this case if you were a judge?

A couple has five children. In this family there are "house rules" for everybody in the house. First: there is no smoking inside the house. Second: There is no cursing and no foul language in the house. One day the children came back from school and told their parents about a student looking for a place to stay and asked their parents if Johnny could stay with them. The parents agreed and Johnny moved in. The parents of the children explained to Johnny the "house rules".

After a few months, Johnny started to smoke and curse in the house. When the father of the children confronted him with the issue, Johnny was angry with everybody in the house. He was asked to leave and he sued the family. When the verdict came in, the family was shocked that the Judge ruled that Johnny's First Amendment rights were abused; that Johnny had a right to curse in any place he wanted (free speech) and that he had the right to smoke in the house. Does that judgment make sense to you? The right of one and last person, who came into the house, trumps the rights of five original members of the house. That is of course ridiculous. That is what happens when a few individuals claim to be atheists, and every existing law in the nation has to be revised to accommodate the few at the expense of the many. Prayers have been said in American schools for years before and after the Amendments to the Constitution. The Founding Fathers, who put the Amendments together, were Christians, who prayed and encouraged that prayers be said in schools. There is no doubt about their belief in God. But for the whims of a few, everybody has to disrespect the symbol of the nation - the American Flag, give up "under God" in the pledge, prayer in school and perhaps "In God we trust" on the money. And where do we stop? Isn't it time for us to stop making the Founding Fathers turn in their graves in disgust?

4. Or the right of the people peaceably to assemble and to petition the Government for a redress of grievances.

As a component of the free speech and free press, the Fathers of the Constitution added that every citizen has the right to demonstrate against the government *peacefully*. This amendment allows citizens to, in a peaceful way express their opinion, disagreement or dissatisfaction of a particular law or person in government, or to call on someone in government to resign. But on no condition should they be allowed to be disrespectful or violent by striking or throwing stones, bottles, raw eggs or other objects on the police or set cars on fire. But what do we see on the streets during demonstrations? Violence! Violence! And more violence! Unfortunately the courts rule that such actions are protected by the First Amendment. Somehow people have forgotten that the important words in this segment of the Constitution are *peaceably* and *grievances*. Nobody is even asking: are these grievances or just perceived grievances? How does one redress what is not even a grievance? The police are there to make sure that the demonstrations are conducted according to the prescriptions of the Constitution. Instead all we see is violence directed on the police. This is what set the freedom marches of Dr. Martin Luther King, Jr. apart from what we see today in the name of freedom of expression.

The First Amendment of the Constitution was and still is a good document only if it is well utilized. The wise Framers knew quite well that religion and politics are all very good tools for man; but the two have to be handled with care and reverence. They are different aspects of man, who is both political and religious. It is for this reason that the idea of separation of Church and State is not only a hoax but does not make sense. Which part of man is religious and which part is political? It would be contradicting God's excellence and wisdom to even suggest that God would create a disjointed human being for the purpose giving him 'freedom'. That would amount to God saying: "Man, when I want you to behave and keep the Ten Commandments is when you are in Church. But when you are in a political environment, you don't need to keep the Commandments." That would be absurd. Where is the integrity of man if he is made to be compartmentalized into 'religious him and political him'? In a "politically correct" mode, a politician has been known to say: "personally I'm against abortion; but as a politician, I have to vote in support of abortion." Yes, he votes to let abortion claim over a million babies in the U.S. every year and on Sunday he goes to Church. If he is Catholic, he goes to receive Holy Communion (the Body and Blood of Christ) and feels he has done his duty to God and humanity. He might stupidly add: "give to Caesar what belongs to Caesar; and God what belongs to God." Come Monday morning, he is ready to empower another High School or College girl to kill her baby with permission and force of law, as if nothing happened, claiming that it was part of the freedom granted by the First Amendment. How about what God said in His Commandment: "Thou shalt not kill"?

CHAPTER FOUR:
ROE V. WADE

According to Supreme Court Justice Blackmun, the right to privacy includes the woman's right to make a decision on abortion and therefore any restriction on this privacy becomes unconstitutional. That is how Justice Blackmun and six other Justices came to the 7-2 decision on Roe v. Wade, which legalized abortion in the United States of America on January 22, 1973. Since then Americans have "legally" killed about 1.3 million babies multiplied by thirty three years since then. That is a whole nation; in fact it is more than some nations. During these years, America has destroyed the equivalent of the total population of Canada and Bolivia combined or the total population of Argentina and Botswana combined. That is a lot of babies. It is amazing that in 33 years, America alone has decimated a population the size of Iraq and Afghanistan combined. On that dark day, January 22, 1973, the one hundred and ninety seven Independent years of American history without legalized abortion was turned upside down by the decision of seven men in black on the Supreme Court of the United States of America. Since then American morality has not been the same.

The introduction of the "pill" and other devices as contraceptive methods was the first step of the "liberation" of American women. It paved the way for the sexual revolution of the sixties. But the contraceptive revolution was not accepted by some women especially among African Americans then. It is a whole other story now among African American women. At that time some of the African American Writers and Community Leaders like Amiri Baraka and Whitney Young respectively, denounced the pill distribution in their communities as an attack on their procreative abilities. Even in the sixties NAACP Leaders in various Branches condemned pill distribution in African American neighborhoods as an act of genocide against them. And they were right. The African Americans of today are worse off because of the introduction of the pill and free abortion services in their neighborhood. The change of attitude of African Americans toward contraception and abortion has harmed their communities very seriously. Not only was it a moral loss on a formerly principled, moral, religious group, which had God to fight their wars over the years of wicked slavery, it was a political loss too. Some "Johnny just come" communities have more political cloud now than African Americans, who have been here for ever. Not realizing that politics is a game of numbers, they hang on to political groups, which give them hand outs, free pills and abortion services. This is freedom, right? Freedom to kill your babies if you want, kill one another in the 'hood', freedom to be promiscuous, do drugs and abuse the ladies! But how did this tragedy come about? It is very difficult to understand that a woman, who is naturally a life-giving and nurturing source, should ask for permission from government to kill her baby in the womb, unless something is terribly wrong somewhere? By this move womanhood lost her femininity. The unnatural act of abortion is itself one of the unfortunate results of contraceptives. The women liberation Movement, Feminism and the Hedonistic Revolution of the sixties: free 'love', sex without consequences or responsibilities, all pleasures and no pain are closely related to the contraceptive culture. With contraceptives on the market, women and sex became free for all "commodities" for men. Closely associated with contraceptives are carelessness and complacency, which in turn lead to unwanted pregnancies. After they got the permission to use contraceptives they found that all is not well yet; there are a lot of pregnancies. Another permission to take care of the pregnancy was requested by women from the United State of America. And they got it in Roe v. Wade. What nobody is telling us is the after effects of contraception and abortion on the woman's body. No one can cheat nature. Contraceptive tablets are drugs used to fool the woman's body in order to prevent pregnancy. When contraceptives tell the body that the woman is already pregnant, conception is prevented. But a woman's bodily cycle is, however interfered with. These interferences, over a period of time, cause other problems like breast cancer in a number of women. The breasts have the obligation to make milk with which to feed the baby afterwards; but there is no real baby. Nature, which is programmed for certain functions, works as if there is a real baby and this is not a good thing; consequently things do go wrong. But nobody talks about these things for so many reasons. We are, nonetheless, paying a heavy price for messing around with nature. It is not politically correct to say these things. But if you want to know more you can go to the internet and do your own research. Go to "The Polycarp Research Institute". You will be amazed at what man has done to woman.

Feminists always talk about how women have, over the years, been exploited by men. This alleged exploitation has been their reason for pushing the "Women Liberation Movement" of the sixties. But unfortunately women have been ten times exploited and enslaved by these women movements. Before women used to be respected by men; today women are more like "sex object" for money. Women have debased women everyday on Television and pages of News Papers and Magazines all over the country for money. Through voluntary indecent exposures and nudity, women further cheapen their womanhood in the name of freedom and liberty to do what they want. If this is not slavery, what else is? That is worse than anything that men did in the past to belittle women. They sale themselves to the public and call it freedom of their bodies and freedom to do what they choose with their bodies. By declaring their independence from men through the feminist movement, they have enslaved themselves over and over again to men to be used by men as slave objects and sex slaves. For a woman to make it in the Entertainment Industry in Hollywood, Las Vegas, or New York, for example, she must be exploited and her woman dignity compromised. That is how her worth in monetary terms is evaluated. What a price to pay for "liberation". Abortion is one such sorry and pitiable "liberation" granted by the United

States Supreme Court to the women of America. Rendering the 7-2 majority opinion in Roe v. Wade (1973), in a 23 page ruling, Justice Harry Blackmun relied heavily on the Griswold v. Connecticut case of 1965. How did Griswold v. Connecticut come about?

One of the general rules in Connecticut against contraceptives says: "Any person who uses drugs, medicinal article or instrument for the purpose of preventing conception shall be fined not less than fifty dollars or imprisoned not less than sixty days or more than one year or be both fined and imprisoned." About accomplices the law states: "Any person who assists, abets, counsels, causes, hires or commands another to commit any offense may be prosecuted and punished as if he were the principal offender." A few individuals did not like this Connecticut law and did everything in their power to repeal it. Two principal agents to take on the State of Connecticut were Griswold, the Executive Director of the Planned Parenthood League of Connecticut, and Buxton, a licensed physician and professor at Yale Medical School. Buxton also served as the medical director for the Planned Parenthood League at its clinic in New Haven. Two other persons in the mix were Fowler Harper, a Yale Law School Professor and Catherine Roraback, a Connecticut attorney. These four people got busy in trying to fight the ban on birth control pills and devices. These attempts started as early as 1958, when the gang of four initiated a series of lawsuits challenging the birth control ban. When they lost, they went to the next level until they succeeded in getting three of their cases to the Connecticut Supreme Court. They lost in all three cases. The desperate activists, who were on a mission, decided to set up a birth control clinic in New Haven, Connecticut in 1961, to try out the ban. Sure enough nine days after, Griswold and Buxton were arrested by Police for violating the birth control law. They were tried and convicted and fined one hundred dollars each. Since they won't quit, they went to the Appellate and finally State Supreme Courts, claiming a violation of their 14th Amendment rights and lost. They went all the way to the United States Supreme Court. In a 7-2 opinion, Griswold and Co. won. Delivering the majority opinion, Justice Douglas, from nowhere, dug up a "privacy right" in the First Amendment to validate their decision. On the other hand, Justice Hugo Black, who served thirty four years in the Supreme

Court, wrote the dissent in Griswold v. Connecticut. He wrote: "The Court talks about a Constitutional right of privacy as though there is some constitutional provision or provisions forbidding any laws ever to be passed which might abridge the privacy of individuals. But there is not." Continuing his dissent Justice Black said: "I realize that many good and able men have eloquently spoken and written about the duty of this court to keep the Constitution in tune with the times. The idea is that the Constitution must be changed from time to time and that this Court is charged with a duty to make those changes. For myself, I must reject that philosophy. The Constitution makers knew the need for change and provided for it. Amendments suggested by the people's elected representatives can be submitted to the people or their selected agents for ratification. That method was good enough for our Fathers, and I must add it is good enough for me." That dissent was good enough for Justice Hugo Black, and it is good enough for me too for whatever it is worth at this stage in the game. A nineteenth century law prohibiting the use of contraceptives was struck down by the Supreme Court in 1965 (Griswold v. Connecticut.). By 1970 contraception was domestically funded by the Federal Government through the Family Planning Services and the so-called Population Research Services Act. In 1971 it went international through the "Foreign Assistance Act". In 1972 the Court went further to extend the sale of contraceptive devices to unmarried people thereby dismantling a Massachusetts' law prohibiting the sale of contraceptive paraphernalia to the unmarried (Eisenstadt v. Baird) The Contraception for Unmarried Persons Case: (1972). In a quick succession acquiring and using contraceptive devices were no longer illegal. That was a shame and the beginning of much more societal confusion, misdirection and problems. There goes another government blunder that created health problems for women. Studies show that women who use pills as a form of contraception have a substantial rise in their high blood pressure and eventual stroke or heart attack. Recently a Channel 7 ABC News carried a segment that some researcher found out that pesticides, washing detergents and some chemicals in the air cause cancer in women by causing chemical imbalance and altering hormones in women. That is an interesting research indeed. One would have thought that the first place to look at when there is a question of hormonal changes or imbalance in women would be in the "contraceptives" they have been taking for years and years. Why do women on contraceptives not get pregnant? Is it not because many of the drugs fool the body cycle of a woman to think that she is already pregnant? In plain language, these drugs alter the body chemistry so that the body cannot produce enough and necessary eggs in the woman to cause pregnancy. It is the imbalance in the hormones that results in no pregnancy. What is up with "some chemicals in the air" that women breathe? That seems to suggest that women have a different air to breathe from the one men breathe. Of course it is politically incorrect to blame it on contraceptives which women have been taking, love to take and will continue to take.

A LITTLE ANALYSIS:

As Justice Hugo Black was suggesting, neither Griswold nor Roe cases has any standing on "privacy" grounds. There is no law made against "privacy". But to link privacy to contraception or abortion rights, is like saying that it is legal for a child molester to go free because he made a private decision and raped a child in the privacy of his home. Having a privacy right to do a crime! Figure that one out. Will anybody buy that? Killing a baby in the womb by itself is *ipso facto* a heinous act and crime. It does not need any other help or declaration to become a crime. The Court ignored the crime of murder and concentrated on privacy of the one perpetrating the crime. You have probably heard the assertion by the group which supports abortion that the government has no business looking into what happens in the privacy of ones home. Based on that assertion, the government would have no business looking into anybody's private home looking for illegal drugs - cocaine, marijuana, Methamphetamine etc - or illegal weapons. It would be unconstitutional for government to clamp down on individuals, who manufacture illegal drugs in their private laboratories in their homes or basements. If the argument made sense, the law Enforcement Officers and Agents would have no jurisdiction going after people with illegal weapons on private properties. Why would Government not respect the privacy rights of individuals, who have chosen to do drugs or prostitute themselves on the streets? That would be "pro-choice", wouldn't it? What do we say about Cops looking for a child who may have been abducted and hidden in the privacy of ones home; or what mandate would the District Attorney have to prosecute a person, who killed his or her spouse in the privacy of his or her home, if we should ignore the real crime and chase after privacy rights of the woman seeking abortion? And the list of crimes goes on. If the government is now desirous to respect the privacy of ones decisions, where do we start and where do we stop? How about the decision, which someone made to jump off the Bay Bridge and die; the decision of someone to ask his Nurse to kill him; the decision and plan to kill another person? These are all private decisions affecting ones self or other individuals' lives. I'm almost certain that everyone, including proponents of abortion, will agree that the government has a right to intervene in the above cited examples because they involve life and death situations just as abortion does. But why would they? It is good to save life. I am sure every one will agree that it is not right for the child molester to rape this child anywhere; it is not right for government to stand idle looking at some one harm himself or kill himself, when perhaps someone could make him feel better about himself and talk him out of killing himself; it would be immoral for government to abandon her job of protecting the people and watch one individual kill another individual or even damage his property. Whether it is protecting people from dangerous drugs, or dangerous weapons, or doing everything to locate, search for and rescue an abducted person, male or female, old or young, it is the right and duty of government. It is even the job of government to make sure that children go to school, even when the parents object to it, because the government understands the adverse consequences in society if these children are not educated. Some private conversations with professionals can be reportable if they endanger the physical or psychological life of a minor. No amount of privacy right can excuse government from doing the right thing. How do these fit into the abortion issue?

Just as voluntarily killing some one is intrinsically evil, whether done publicly or privately, killing someone in the womb is intrinsically evil. When privacy right clashes with a morally bad act, the avoidance of the morally bad action wins over individual privacy. Who did it or where it is done has no relevance in the case.

Here is an example to illustrate this issue: It belongs under ones privacy boundaries to eat meat or fish every day or once a week or a month or a year or none at all; an individual has the right to buy this car or that one or none at all. It is ones privacy right to dye ones hair any color one wants, even though ones friends may not like it. And the list goes on. But it is not within ones privacy rights to steal some one's car or money or any kind of property. There are rights, and there are *rights*. It was an unfortunate decision for the Supreme Court to make the killing of 1.3 million innocent babies a year in the United States legal on the basis of a woman's right. Call it any thing you want but don't call it "privacy rights". *I call it killing of innocent babies, who did not ask to be conceived.*

When Norma Mc Corvey alias, Jane Roe in Roe v Wade, a pregnant woman from Dallas, challenged the Texas Penal Code against abortion, which prohibition was in existence in 32 other States, and filed a law suit in 1970 in the District Court for the Northern District of Texas and saw herself in the hands of two women attorneys, who were desirous to get an opportunity to challenge the Texas abortion law. Linda Coffee and Sarah Weddington were thrilled with an opportunity, which they were looking for. On behalf of Norma, they requested for an injunction to make Texas authority stop prosecuting women who committed abortion. This was denied by the three-Justice District Court. Consequently Jane Roe and the others who rejected appellate Court's decision went to the Supreme Court.

Writing the majority opinion, Justice Harry Blackmun relied on the "privacy right" of Griswold v. Connecticut to conclude that a woman has a privacy right to terminate her pregnancy. Ironically but rightly he started with this statement: "The Constitution does not explicitly mention any right of privacy." You got that right, Justice. But he presented his main thesis thus: "This right of privacy, whether it be founded in the Fourteenth Amendment's concept of personal liberty, as we feel it is, or, as the District Court determined, in the Ninth Amendment's reservation of rights to the people, is broad enough to encompass a woman's decision whether or not to terminate her pregnancy." Based on this statement, nobody would obey the laws of the States or the Federal Government because all laws touch on or contradict someone's privacy or "liberty", one way or the other. There is no dispute as to the validity of the privacy of every individual. The problem is how to make sure that the privacy law made by human beings gives way to a higher law made by God Himself. Justice Blackmun and his colleagues failed to see that the right to live is by far superior to the privacy right of an individual to have fun because a dead person cannot have privacy. One must first be alive in order to ask for rights. Aborted babies did not have the opportunity to ask for the "right to terminate a pregnancy".

Again this individual had the "right to choose" and he/she chose to engage in a sexual activity, *which by nature is capable of resulting into a child being brought into th*e *world*. That is how we all came into this world. It is not fair for this individual (the mother) to deprive that other individual (the unborn) his or her right to live in order to satisfy a selfish end. That unborn baby's life is far more important than any other individual's private joys or freedom. Unfortunately by abortion, this action can be repeated over and over again with private and public funds. Is this what the Founding Fathers of this Great Nation intended by the Ninth and Fourteenth Amendments? The fact of the matter is that the so-called privacy law as applied in Griswold v. Connecticut as well as Roe v. Wade is not in the Constitution. It was forced in by Justice Blackmun and six other Justices in order to use privacy in the two cases. And that is a tragedy. In a lot of ways, this looks like a scene taken from ones dream or Holly-Wood horror movie. It is scary.

Let us give Justice Blackmun and Co. the benefit of the doubt in the first premise, that the so-called "right of privacy" is founded on the 14th Amendment's "concept of personal liberty". How does that translate into killing another human being? Does a woman now have the "liberty" to get rid of any person on her way to realize her personal liberty? In other words, because a woman has a right to exercise her liberty, she can also take away the liberty of her baby to live? The strongest argument people make in support of privacy is that the State has no right to look into people's bedrooms to know what they are doing. What if a child molester takes his victim to his bedroom, should the State steer clear because he is operating within the confines and privacy of his bedroom? Of course not! The State has a right to violate the privacy guarantees for a higher cause, namely the kidnapped child, who might loose his life if time is wasted. In the same token, the interest of the unborn baby should truncate any other consideration. With all due respect to a Justice of the Supreme Court, it is as illogical as it is callous to give a woman permission to kill her baby because she has the liberty under the 14th Amendment to do so. It has been suggested that the mother is the only person at play in a pregnancy. That again is nonsensical. How about the baby? What is a woman pregnant with? Is she pregnant with nobody or somebody; a person or a soccer ball? Even then a soccer ball is something. If the fusion of the man's sperm and the woman's egg (fetus) is nothing, why do women, in the first few weeks of their pregnancies, announce to their Moms, and friends that they are expecting a baby? Some women in the excitement start to buy clothes and cots for the baby and sometimes they paint the baby's room a certain favorite color. They start to discuss what name to give the baby in the womb. I guess that is not politically correct to say or do. Why do people play "head games" with something as serious as life, a baby's life? Some have argued that the "fetus" is not a baby and not a person. What is a person? What are the essential properties of a person? What is lacking in the so-called "tissue" (as some people refer to the fetus), which if you let it, comes out after 9 months as a baby? If the fetus is left alone, it is a dynamic organism that is growing like any other organism in nature even as the conversation goes on about how to get rid of him. It is a pity that abortion rights activists say that life does not begin at conception. The question then is: When does it begin? Is it after birth, or a few hours or weeks before birth? Who will tell the world when life begins in a pregnant woman's womb? Can anyone in good conscience say they don't know when life begins? And what is life? When does "life begin in anything that has life? The woman knows that "something" is happening inside her. Or should we continue to put the blinders on because of pleasure and selfishness in perpetuation of the carnage of abortion and political correctness, which have engulfed the Nation? Should we continue, every year, to deny 1.3 million American babies their right to live as we are living? Barbarians do not even kill their kind like we do, a "civilized" nation.

Or are those babies not our kind? May be they are just tissues which after years *will continue* to be the same tissues indefinitely.

But the fact is that the fetus has, within its composition, its own DNA different from that of the mother; it has an individuating principle, which makes it unique and separates it from anybody else; it develops with its own organs, with a heart that beats, as ultra sound machines have revealed. With the help of advanced Science, we know that it is a human being that is murdered in every abortion even in the early months of the pregnancy. Quoting from KOOP, "Right to Live", John J. Davis in his book, Evangelical Ethics, wrote: "eighteen to twenty days after conception, the baby's heart is already beating because the heart is the center of this machine called human being. At eight weeks brain waves can be detected and finger prints have already formed. By the ninth and tenth weeks, the thyroid and adrenal glands are functioning, and the child can squint, swallow, and move the tongue. By the twelve and thirteenth weeks, the child can suck his thumb and recoil from pain if pricked with a needle. (First Trimester- and he can be pricked or forced out of the womb) By the fourth month the unborn child is eight to ten inches in height." The words in brackets are mine. So what is Justice Blackmun talking about a woman's "personal liberty" in the Fourteenth Amendment when we should be talking about the personal liberty of her baby too? With all these functions of a baby in the womb, would abortion activists agree that life has begun? Of course not! According to Susan M. Ludington, an assistant professor of nursing at UCLA, numerous studies have shown that the unborn can respond to different colors of light directed toward the mother's belly, and to different types of music. "We now know that from about 17 to 24 weeks, gestation age, all systems are operational. The baby does respond, and early learning can occur," said Ludington. Abortion goes on in this Country up to the second and third trimesters in "partial-birth abortions".

If the second premise in Justice Blackmun's argument is true, namely that this right of privacy was founded on the 9th Amendment's reservation of rights to the people, why would Judge Blackmun and his six other Justices and supporters take it upon themselves to be "the People" to give women the permission to decide whether or not to terminate their pregnancies? Who made these judges "the people"?

One would expect that the matter would have been left for "the people" of the United States of America to decide through their Legislators or through a plebiscite. This decision by the seven Justices in the United States Supreme Court is a typical example of 'judicial activism', which is, in itself unconstitutional and a manifestation of arrogance on their part. Since when has it been constitutional and legal to give free choice to people to commit an offence in the name of "privacy rights"? In Roe v. Wade, women were given the permission to choose whether to terminate their pregnancy (kill the unborn) or not. Why did the Justices not give the same "freedom of choice" to men and women to choose to marry more than one partner at the same time; why did they not give to drug addicts the freedom of choice to quit or continue to do illegal drugs without harassment; why not let people have the permission to choose to kill or not to kill their neighbors, spouses and anyone else they can kill; why did the seven Justices not give people the permission to steal or not to steal; to let teens have the "freedom of choice" to drink hard liquor or not? And the list goes on and on with every crime on the books today. I don't think anyone doubts that teenagers have rights too. If teenage girls (13 – 17) have the "choice" to terminate their pregnancy without parental consent, why should they not have the same choice to consume alcohol and do drugs if they choose to? Where did the seven Justices in Roe v. Wade and those in Congress, who support them today, draw the line of "privacy" and "right"? It makes perfect sense and perfect logic to continue dishing out "rights" and "freedoms" irrespective of who is hurt. Is there any wonder why teens in our society today don't take adults seriously because adults like the seven Justices in Roe v. Wade are full of contradictions? Teens hear one thing today, and tomorrow they hear a contradictory message. They are told not to drink, smoke or engage in illicit sexual behaviors by adults and they turn around to say: "Look who's talking". Again the right of the people concept used in reference to the Ninth Amendment to justify abortion, does not fit into any reasonable category.

In rendering the majority opinion, Justice Blackmun did however say:

"It is reasonable and appropriate for a State to decide that at some point in time another interest, that of the health of the mother or that of potential life, becomes significantly involved. The woman's privacy is no longer sole and any right of privacy she has must be measured accordingly." This sounds like Pilate condemning Jesus to die and turn around and wash his hands off the blood of an "innocent man". It is too late, Justice Blackmun and company. The gin is already out of the bottle. Thanks and no thanks to you! The damage is already done.

By this law the Court has taken the role of the Legislators. Justice Rehnquist put it very well in his dissent:

"The decision here to break pregnancy into three distinct terms and to outline the permissible restrictions the State may impose in each one, for example, partakes more of judicial legislation than it does of a determination of the intent of the drafters of the Fourteenth Amendment." The seven Justices were not interpreting the law; instead they set forth some periods in the pregnancy when the State can come in (after the first trimester) to make laws prohibiting abortion. But recently the Court has ruled in favor of abortion into the second and third trimesters until the Republicans in Congress pushed and passed a bill prohibiting "Partial Birth Abortion" which involves a gruesome dismemberment of a new-born baby. Since the abortionists do not want to kill a human being outside the womb, the doctor uses a syringe or any pointed object to perforate the baby's head (skull) to let the baby die before he/she fully comes out. Hence the name is 'partial birth' abortion. The doctors don't want to go through criminal proceedings if they kill the baby after birth. So they kill the baby half way before birth. Sometimes the abortion doctors and nurses are embarrassed when a supposedly dead baby, after he has been poisoned in the womb, comes out alive. To save face with a "clear conscience", they will leave the baby unaided to die. That way they, like Pilate, could wash their hands off the death of an innocent child.

With regard to the issue of whether or not the unborn is a human being with legal rights, the majority opinion claimed that it did not belong to the judiciary to dabble into the issue of when life begins. W-h-a-o! Interesting realization! One would expect that before a far-reaching pronouncement is made about taking away the life of the unborn, the Justices would have had the good sense to find out if "this thing" in the womb has life or not; legal rights or not. If this thing in the womb has life, when did it start? Instead they pushed the buck to the "States" to see when the "woman's privacy is no longer sole". All of a sudden the seven Justices realized that there is something in the womb which they referred to as "potential life". That is very convenient, to say the least, for the seven Justices to get off easily like that. It appears that these Justices knew that they *forced* the privacy issue into the Roe v. Wade case. Justice Blackmun had some problems coming to terms with the ultimate decision. Somehow it looked like he owed something to those agitators. It was said that he came up with this privacy theory at the very last moment. Hence he and his fellows tried to do a damage control by injecting the idea of the States' intervention in determining when "the woman's privacy is no longer sole" and the "potential life" could be given some recognition. That is ridiculous. It is even more atrocious to continue to uphold and defend a law that is intrinsically wrong. But because it has to do with women, abortion will have to be continued especially when the men are not complaining.

Two conscientious Justices dissented in Roe v. Wade. The first was Justice Byron White and the second was Justice William Rehnquist, the most junior of the justices at the time. But he later became the Chief Justice of the Supreme Court. Justice Byron White was afraid of the "Court" becoming a super legislature. He saw the majority opinion as "illegitimate" because he could not find any justification in the Constitution for legalizing abortion. In their book ROE V. WADE, The Abortion Rights Controversy in American History, N. E. H. Hull and Peter Charles Hoofer described White's dissent thus: "The Court's majority had turned women's 'whim or caprice' into a constitutional principle, although there was nothing in the Constitution's language to sustain that judgment. To convenience a mother, and for little more, the Court had 'disentitled' the legislators of all fifty states from weighing the 'relative importance of the continued existence and development of the fetus on the one hand against a spectrum of possible impacts on the mother on the other hand.'" In his own dissent Justice Rehnquist rightly claimed that Ms. Roe was not pregnant at the time the decision was rendered; consequently the Court had overreached itself in giving her a relief she did not need and could not claim because she had given birth to her baby. Secondly he contended that there was no privacy right involved in the abortion issue because it was not a private act.

But arguing her case before the Supreme Court in favor of abortion and on behalf of Roe, Attorney Sarah Waddington said: "It (referring to her client's pregnancy) disrupts her body, it disrupts her education, it disrupts her employment, and it often disrupts her entire family life...and because of the impact on the woman, this certainly, in as far as there are any rights which are fundamental, is a matter...of such fundamental and basic concern to the woman involved that she should be allowed to make the choice as to whether to continue or terminate her pregnancy." As Justice Rehnquist said in his dissent, Roe had given birth to her baby and the case had no more legal standing. With regard to all the so-called disruptions mentioned, some are natural consequences of being pregnant and others had no reasonable standing at all. How does pregnancy disrupt education when millions of pregnant women go to school and work or continue school and work after childbearing? How does being pregnant disrupt a woman's "entire life"? Pregnancy is not a disease. It is natural. All over the world, there are millions of women, who are pregnant and happy. There was no evidence before the Court to show that Roe was raped. It was like purposely jumping into the sea in Alaska on a winter morning and turn around to complain that the water was cold. Or one could describe it as an adult sticking his finger into boiling water and turn around and complain to every body that the water was hot and burned his finger. Hello-o o-o o! Welcome to the real world, Attorney Waddington. She should have known that pregnancy could occur when a woman decides to have sex with a man. Once again the seven Justices listened and bought the "disruption" story by Roe's attorney. Did the story end there? Of course not!

Planned Parenthood was not satisfied with their victory over the killing of defenseless children. Based on the public outcry of the people about the number of abortions taking place in the State, the Pennsylvanian Legislature passed a Bill to control abortion in the State called "Abortion Control Act" of 1982, nine years after Roe v. Wade. It came about when people got tired of seeing so many innocent babies being killed with reckless abandon. The "Control Bill" had five components:

a.) It required that a woman seeking an abortion give an informed consent and be given some information about the "before and after" of abortion at least twenty four hours before the abortion takes place.

b.) If it is a minor, it required that one of the parents must give consent before the abortion, with the understanding that the courts could over ride it in very special circumstances, which were also specified in the Bill.

c.) It stipulated that the above could be bye-passed in cases of "medical emergency", which is also defined in the Bill.

d.) If the woman is married, she must sign that she informed her husband about the abortion.

e.) The abortion clinics must do some kind of reporting of their activities.

The abortionists did not like these restrictions. They filed a suit challenging them in Planned Parenthood of Southern Pennsylvania v. Casey in July of '82. The District Court agreed with them completely. The Appellate Court disagreed with the abortion doctors except the notification of husband by the wife clause. In other words, the Appellate Court agreed that a woman could commit an abortion without the knowledge of her husband. However it went up to the Supreme Court, which disagreed with the two lower courts. It must be mentioned here that at this time around, three of the Roe V. Wade Justices had retired. The majority opinion was written by three Justices: Anthony Kennedy, David Souter and Sandra Day O'Connor. They, in effect said that abortion is still legal before the viability of the fetus. (Whatever they meant by "viability"!) They also reiterated the power of the States to restrict abortion after "viability". Finally they went back to the important point that the State has an important job of protecting the pregnant mother and her fetus. This is a bit ambiguous. The fetus is nothing on the one hand, and again, it is something on the other and needs protection. This is trying to placate both sides of the debate. Of course this is a modified court from the original Roe v. Wade court. It reminds me of the Solomon case in the Bible, where the woman who stole another woman's baby and was caught agreed to a proposal to spilt the baby into two.

Talking about "viability", do you know any child born after nine months under normal delivery and left all alone in a room and is viable? It is disingenuous if not deceptive to be throwing out words like viability to defend the defenseless. Every human being, "ab initio" to old age, needs help to function. If a child such as this cannot be viable, how can we expect a child three months in the womb to be judged on the basis of viability in order to be given a shot at life? Even a grown up adult, an old and handicapped person will not be viable without some help from other people. We need patience to be ready for some things to let other things happen. Everybody needs some assistance to perform some duties. One can be breathing and still cannot survive without the help of others or others being patient with the individual to produce some result. That is why a child in the womb, at any stage of development, needs the full term to be born. We are all for Americans with Disabilities Act (ADA) laws, that protect a certain segment of our population. Unfortunately it is the same people, who rightly advocate for the protection of some people in our society, who cannot function at the same rate as everyone else, who are not willing to give the unborn some time, three, four, five or six more months to develop into a healthy baby in somebody's arms. Instead for the *convenience* of the mother, for whatever other reason - shame, economic conditions, dislike for children, discomfort with pregnancy or whatever else - pro-abortion Americans disinherit millions of babies every year in America. America frowns at any person, who discriminates against Senior Citizens on the basis of shame, economics, dislike for old age, or the discomfort of dealing with them at different crossroads of life. But the same America will not stand up with one voice to condemn the killing of innocent babies. Why would the same people stand for the rights of poor and marginalized people and ignore the right of babies in the womb to be born? Unless people are allowed to be born, they have no other rights. They don't have the right to vote, to receive hand out, to receive welfare benefits, subsidized housing, cutting their taxes down. They are dead because you condemned them. Can you imagine the ruckus that would ensue if one aborts the baby of one of the so-called "Endangered Species" of animals in the wild? The heavens would be turned upside down. It is ironic that it is the same abortionists and abortion advocates, who happen to be Animal Activists too. It is unfortunate that there are some people, who would prefer to save so-called endangered species to saving a baby in the womb. They are the same people who don't want to have children but they have twenty cats and half a dozen dogs. They love animals because they don't talk back to you. It is a shame that we have degenerated to the level that even Learned Jurists would call the killing of innocent babies, a First Amendment Right of Privacy when it is not so. So help us God.

It must be noticed here that a life issue is here being played with as a game, which politicians engage in. First of all, how much trust should we have in these Judges? Since January 22, 1973, a set of Judges from the States to the Federal say that it is completely the right of a woman to kill the fetus in her womb with no questions asked if she so desires. Some, on the other hand, believe that life begins at conception and nobody has a right to interfere with the fetus; another set of Judges, over the years, says they cannot know when life begins and still talk of "viability". Some Judges believe that abortion is fine and legal but should be discretionary.. Even among those Judges, who believe they can live with abortion being legal, we have some, who think that the woman should be given enough knowledge about the consequences of abortion, before, during, and after, as well as parental and husband notifications. There are some Justices, who still don't think a husband has a say on whether or not *his child* is aborted, while some believe that the States have an obligation to protect a pregnant woman and the baby inside of her. Are all these men and women looking at the same Constitution and Amendments? Just imagine that these are the people, who are supposed to objectively decide cases. God save us.

A lot of Women Organizations have done a disservice to womanhood. The basest of them all is that women have championed and still continue till today to champion the cause of violence on innocent children in the womb. Women went from being known as nurturers of life to destroyers of life. The woman is no longer the protector of babies. She ceases to be the safe container of babies. If a baby is no longer safe with her Mom, where else can he run for shelter and safety? He is not safe with the abortion doctor, who took "the Hippocratic oath" to protect and save life; the baby is not safe with the nurse in the abortion clinic; and he is not even safe with his own flesh and blood, his mom. It is cold; it is tragic; it is horrible. It is uncivilized. Barbarians would hesitate to kill their flesh and blood. The women leaders in the Feminist Movements and Planned Parenthood are the advocates of this assault on American children. To deceive people these Feminist Groups have come up with misleading slogans referring to abortion as "pro-choice" instead of "calling a spade a spade". It is "pro-abortion", plain and simple. In the context of abortion, "pro choice" is a misnomer. It is very ingenious on the part of abortionists to spin on that word. Pro-choice is a terminology that is mild and also indifferent to the reality of what is really going on. It is an ingenious choice because it well hides the facts and deceives a lot of people about abortion. The fact of the matter is that every human being is pro-choice. There are so many things human beings have a choice in. Every one has a choice in deciding to eat out or at home; to smile or not to smile; to run or walk; to vote in an election or not to vote (if one is a citizen); to watch the games or to read, etc. But there are some things human beings do not have any choice in. We do not choose our parents. We do not have a choice to kill them either without a drastic consequence; we do not have a choice to marry our children; we do not have a choice to drive on the left side of the road in America and some other countries that drive on the right without a "ticket", etc. So for a group to describe the choice to kill a baby as "Pro-choice" is deceptive, to put it mildly. That legal abortion ever started and continues to go on today is the design of these dangerous women. It shows forth the proof that women can also have the "heart of stone". In Macbeth, William Shakespeare puts it this way about a woman, who had a heart of stone:

"That one could smile and smile and still be a villain". And "Cruelty, thy name is woman."

Another self-deception is when women claim that no one can tell them what to do with their own body or their reproductive system. That in itself is a bunch of baloney and nonsense. If one wants to look at it from a spiritual point of view, the body is not their own; it belongs to God. And on the natural level, everybody is a part of the community of people with laws and regulations involving a series of give and take. No one is an island; that is why we have laws to protect everyone's interest and still have *some* individual freedom. Everyday we go about obeying rules and being told what to do. From the house where we live we are told what to do by practically everybody and everything in the house. We do not run anything except our mouths. From the light switch to the cooking stove to the recipe to driving out of the garage, we are following orders. We drive on the right side of the street because someone tell us to do so; we get down to work we are following orders for as many hours we work. Uncle Sam directs our movement and how we spend. Yet someone will have the mouth to say she does not want somebody to tell her what to do with her body. This is outright stupidity and arrogance. How then is a woman's body hers, to the point that the government cannot have a say in what she does with it especially, when there is a third party, the baby, who has rights too as an American? The baby in the womb has a different DNA from his mother. How does she have a right to her own body and also usurp the right of the baby? The State has an obligation to protect the third party. If we accept that nobody has a right to tell a woman not to kill the baby in her womb, why does the State government stop people who want to jump off the bridge from doing so? Why does the government spend billions of dollars trying to stop people who like to put dangerous drugs into *their bodies*? Why do we prosecute and imprison such people if we recognize that women have the right to kill their babies simply because the bodies are theirs? Why does Government imprison a twenty year old adult for having consensual sex with a sixteen year old (Statutory Rape)? The bodies are theirs and the reproductive systems are theirs too, according to these ladies and their supporters. Why does government arrest someone, who wants to walk the streets nude? Where is the so-called "Freedom of Choice"? After all, the body is his or hers. We do all these and more to save people and lives. Yet killing innocent babies is far more serious a crime than smoking weed, for which the Government puts thousands of people in prisons every year. There are too many contradictions in the affairs of government: the government has a right to interfere with people's lives and bedrooms (bugging homes and businesses, paying unscheduled visits to child molesters' and rapists' homes. And parolees go through the same routine and if they violate them they may be punished by jail and or prison sentence;

and at the same time government does not have a right to look into people's "bed rooms", a terminology often used by pro-abortionists.

Before 1965, the use of contraceptives was illegal in the United States of America. When the use of contraceptives became legal in 1965, the next logical thing to follow was abortion in 1973, less than ten years after the legalization of contraceptives. With the introduction of contraceptives, promiscuity naturally was intensified. Irresponsible, casual and careless sexual activities became frequent and an acceptable norm backed up by legislation. As we know accidents happen out of carelessness; there were unwanted pregnancies here and there because men and women, even teens did not have to think twice or worry about the consequences of having sex especially out of wedlock. The next logical thing after pregnancy occurs was to ask for abortion on demand. All these are riding under the "privacy" interpretation of Griswold v. Connecticut. Will it stop there? Not at all; Assisted-suicide has become legal in some of the States. Any surprises? There shouldn't be. After all, the babies in the womb are described as "unwanted". Some people regard old and sick people as unwanted and useless. That is why they have to be killed. What do you expect? The baby in the womb is not able to work and earn a living. He is a liability and disruptive to her mother who would like to be out and about with men having "fun". And so the law says we can kill him. So is the old lady, who is no longer productive; the law again says we can kill her. As a nation we are being hostile to the very young and the very old in society and we were in the womb, and young; we may probably get old..

Sodomy Laws have been abrogated, and gay marriages are also legal in some States of the Union. Like abortion, it is convenient to have homosexual relationships without having to worry about any consequences or responsibilities of the action. It is amazing that in 2005, California, where the voters earlier rejected "same sex marriage" in Proposition #22, the Democratic led State Legislature, with a few gays and lesbians of its own, passed Assembly Bill 849, which would legalize same-sex "marriage" in the State. The State Governor threatened to veto the bill through his Press Secretary, Margita Thompson: "Only marriage between a man and a woman is valid or recognized in California. We cannot have a system where the people vote and the Legislature derails that vote. Out of respect for the will of the people, the Governor will veto AB 849." And he did veto the Bill. The Griswold ill-wind, which was set in motion in 1965, is still blowing ill-wind and is still waxing strong. What will be next? With one fundamental mistake in 1965, there have been a series of bad and misleading laws and the people of the United States are the worst for it. Who knows what's next?

According to a weekly publication, Culture & Cosmos, July 26, 2005 Issue, 53% of women who had unintended pregnancies used a contraceptive method during the month they got pregnant. In an article in Washington Post, Black and Hispanic women have higher abortions of 32% and 20% respectively. There are higher abortion rates among low income women and women on Medicaid. Why? It is free, of course. About 60% of women who had abortions in the year 2000 had income below $28,000 per year for a family of three. They didn't have to pay; with tax payers' money, we encourage them. Considered in age groups, 56% of the women who terminated their pregnancies were in their twenties while those from fifteen to nineteen account for only 19%. Why? It is probably because most in this age bracket are still living with Mom and Dad while a good portion of the 56% group will probably be students in College living outside the home. They are now free as a bird plus the fact that they receive free student services on campus. You can't beat that. As long as we are ready to pay, they are ready to oblige us.

Abortionists target teenage girls in High Schools for abortion through the instrumentality of School Authorities, Nurses and Counselors. They take students from school to abortion clinics without parental notification. As if that is not enough, Activist judges rule that such students have a Constitutional right to abortion without parental notification. Can anything be more bizarre and absurd than that? It is the same Courts that enforce the law that minors cannot drive; they can't go to Casinos to play; cannot drink alcohol legally, cannot vote and much more. It is the same Courts, which rule that minors cannot be given any form of medication in school without notifying at least one of the parents first, if they get sick in school. If any student broke something in school, parents are notified immediately. He or she cannot be completely held accountable because he or she is a minor.

I guess a broken object is more important than a baby in the womb. If a student is to be suspended for a day from school, at least one of his parents is invited to the school for it. But killing a baby in the womb of a minor with the help of school authorities is done without informing the parents. What a justice in the Justice System! It was a big surprise to witness the Parental Notification Initiative, called Proposition 73 fail in California in November 7, 2005 Elections. It was not only Judges, who failed the children; the people of California also failed them. The madness has really caught on. We have all been addicted to abortion, it seems. Lord, have mercy.

CHAPTER FIVE:
NIGERIAN FREEDOMS

Nigeria has been and still is a Secular State. There was, of course, an attempt by President Sani Abacha, a former Military Head of State, to secretly introduce or register Nigeria as a member of the Organization of Islamic Countries (OIC). The attempt was nipped in the bud as soon as it came to light by a Foreign Newspaper. The people of Nigeria were outraged. Local newspapers and the people with one voice forced Abacha to withdraw the application. He said he put Nigeria in as an observer nation. It was clear from the beginning of the republic that Nigeria has a good number of religions with over two hundred language groups. Since she became an Independent Country on October 1, 1960, different religious groups have freely and appreciably exercised their religious rights without any governmental molestation. The major religions are Islam, Christianity and varied indigenous religions. There are probably other small religious groups as one can find in almost any other country of multi ethnic groups. There seems to be mutual respect among the different groups. There have been, however, a few times in the recent history when some Shiite Moslems from a neighboring Country came and disrupted the religious and peaceful balance in Nigeria. They set some Christian Churches on fire and the Christians retaliated by setting some Mosques on fire too. The Federal Government came in and quelled the problem. Apart from those isolated cases, there is a good-neighborly understanding between the different religions. The

Government intervention in the above-mentioned cases shows that the Government enforces and supports the freedom of religion as is enshrined in the Nigerian Constitution. It is the expectation of the people that their Governments, Local, State and Federal, encourage and support religion because they understand the advantages and influence of religion in people's lives. The Leaders are not hostile to religion as is the case in the United States of America. Instead the Nigerian Government encourages the practice of religion.

Before the Nigerian – Biafra war, there were only a couple of Universities and a few Government Teacher Training Colleges and High Schools in Nigeria. While there were no Religious/Mission Universities then, there were many Religious Teacher Training Colleges and High Schools in the Nation. The bulk of the Nigerian Elite were the product of Christian Schools. The Missionaries brought education along with religion just as the Colonialists brought education with politics. That arrangement introduced western religion and religious practices into the schools. To teach in a Protestant School, one must be a practicing Protestant. One has to be a Catholic in good standing to teach in a Catholic School because the teacher had to impart academic as well as religious education and principles. In order to be a teacher of the Koranic school, one must be a good Muslim. That guaranteed that the subject matter was well transmitted. In the end the moral tone of each religious group was safeguarded and parents were assured that their wards were getting a comprehensive, well-rounded education, which was actually pure academics and good spirituality. There we have a good standard of education and a healthy association in the schools and the society.

The Nigerian – Biafra war lasted for 30 months before Biafra surrendered. The Nigerian side of the war thought that the conflict would last for a few weeks. The Nigerian Military President then, General Yakubu Gowon called the Biafra attempt a "police action", which would be quelled in a matter of weeks. When it did not happen that way and the war lasted for thirty months, someone had to be blamed. They blamed the long duration of the war on the help from Caritas International, Oxfam and the World Council of Churches, which sent a lot of food, clothing and medical relief to Biafra. As a punishment, the Federal Government of Nigeria ordered the repatriation of all Missionary Priests and Nuns, who were primarily Irish Holy Ghost Fathers and Holy Rosary Sisters, who were mostly in the heart of Biafra. In furtherance to the repatriation of the Missionaries, the Administrators appointed by the Federal Government in the Biafra-run territories were instructed to take over all the Missionary Schools. Their names were all changed from Saints' names like St. Jude's High School to City, Village or Local names to efface their religious origin. Other non Catholic religious and private schools were also taken by the State Government order.

That attempt was to weaken the religious influence in the lives of the people. It did not quite work that way. The Military people made a big mistake. There were lots of bad signs with the schools' take over. Immediately they saw that the absence of God in the now Government run School system was already having devastating effects on their ability to run the Country. The schools were like what we have in any public school in the United States now with regard to violence, drugs and indiscipline introduced by young boys, who came back from the Army to finish up school from where they left off before the war. The challenge was too much for the Government to handle. They invited the Religious Leaders to strike an accord. There was a compromise. Religion was reintroduced in the Schools. The study of the Bible and Islamic studies once more became part of the curricula. The religious subjects attained equal status with History, English, Mathematics, and the Sciences. Students had the option of choosing to study the Bible, Islamic studies or none of them. Talking about freedom, that was real religious freedom. The religious Leaders pressed further to get the actual doctrinal moral teachings in schools within school hours. It is a fact that students spend more time in school than they spend with their parents. In all the schools in the Federation, different religious Leaders: Catholic Priests, Protestant Ministers of all denominations, Imams etc are free to come into these State owned and run Schools and teach their doctrines to their adherents for one hour every week, provided they teach students of their religion or denomination in the school they visit. It was to be voluntary too for students and teachers to attend. There again we see freedom in action not just a slogan. It was agreed that Thursdays would be the day. Before the Ministers or Religious

Leaders or their representatives arrive, some of the teachers would arrange the students according to their religious or denominational faith groups. The teachers are free to attend the teachings, Religious Services or Masses. This is also optional for students and teachers. But it is available and above all, official. There is no so-called separation of Church and State in Nigeria because the people and government understand that no one can really separate Church and State. That again is what Freedom of Religion is about. This has been in place in Nigeria since after the end of the war in the early seventies. People were not expected to deny their faith because they were on State grounds as it is in the United States. In Nigerian schools, it is still standard to have what is generally called "Morning Assembly" where students and staff gather together and offer some prayers to begin the day. This worship service sets the tone of the day and can be led by the Principal of the school, any staff member or the school Senior Prefect or anyone he or she may call upon to lead the prayers for that day. This is followed by a song and announcements for the day. At the close of day, dismissal is done with prayer from the Assembly ground with a few announcements for the next day. In over thirty years of practice, no one has complained about God or prayer in schools. Expressions of prayer are not considered out of place by the Nigerian people. The Nigerian people would not let any group like "American Civil Liberties Union" to misguide or misdirect the people in matters affecting the worshipping of God or teaching of religion in schools. One can see how ridiculous it is to even suggest that voluntary prayer in a public place violates the "establishment of religion" clause of the First Amendment. It is here that America can learn one or two things that are working from the Nigerian people. The Separation of Church and State tactics is flawed because students praying in school does not equate to establishing a national religion. Nigeria does not have a national religion. This seems to show that Nigerians know the difference between *individuals' practice of their religion, which the First Amendment protects and encourages in America, and the State establishment of religion, which the First Amendment prohibits.* Individuals and or groups of people practicing their religion anywhere in the country does not mean that the nation has established a national religion for all to practice. Why is this simple fact too hard for some people to comprehend? It is the projection of the will of a few, who do not believe in God for whatever reason we don't care to know. If there is someone, who does not believe in God, no one is or should force him to pray or believe in God. But his will or desire should not trump the will or desire of the majority. After all, when the majority elects a President, Governor or any elected official he or she becomes everybody's President or Governor or Representative. He/she is not just for those who voted for him/her. The will of the majority is respected. In a school Assembly prayer, a student is free not to take part in the prayer.

One of the fears of this writer is that Nigeria could lose this nice thing going for her if she is not careful about how she swallows everything from the United States of American culture. It only takes a few learned gentlemen and ladies with American training to import the American so-called "Separation of Church and State" doctrine or "Freedom of Speech" American style, into the Nigerian educational system. Cursed be that day because it would have a devastating effect on students and parents, and of course, the entire society. It is getting to be a little tough being religious there when religion is taught in schools now; only God knows what will happen if the so-called separation of Church and State doctrine is introduced into the Nigerian educational system. God forbid!

Pro "Choice" (Pro-Abortion) In Nigeria???:

All over the world, from time immemorial, different peoples and cultures have experienced individual women commit abortion secretly, so have people committed fratricide, matricide, patricide, and adultery; people have told lies and people have stolen privately and have tried to keep them secret and that has made these actions rare. Some of these people probably regarded these actions of murdering their fellow human beings, committing adultery, lying or stealing, acts of bravery or smartness. But why do they always do them in secret? It is amazing that, with one voice, most of these cultures regard these actions as wrong or anti-social behaviors, at least. In that regard one can say that Nigeria has her share of these behaviors either as individuals or groups. Those behaviors have always been seen as crimes in Nigeria even when some people might be secretly doing them as you read this. People steal everyday, yet stealing is still a crime. People die everyday killing or trying to kill others or committing other crimes; yet killing is still a crime.

Freedom is a universal concept stemming from its source, God. President Bush, (forty three) has said so many times that Freedom is God's gift to humanity. Nigerians understand fully well that the "freedom" of a mother to kill her baby, is no freedom at all because it does not come from God. From the major indigenous religions to other forms of religious expressions in Nigeria, abortion has always been regarded as wrong and sinful even though some people still do it. Therefore it has not been legalized in Nigeria. Making something legal by a Nation or State is giving its seal of approval that this thing or action is good and or authorized. It is the national authorization to do evil acts that tips the balance in legalization of abortion. As unsophisticated as the people are, compared to the American society, they still know that life begins at conception and anyone who interferes with the fetus is regarded as a child killer. Among the indigenous people, even before the advent of Christianity, any "medicine man" who attempted to terminate a pregnancy, is severely punished. His action is described in the indigenous religions as an **abomination, a desecration of the "land or earth goddess"**; an upset of the equilibrium of the earth and an interference with the fertility goddess. The desecration of the land constitutes an offence against the deity. Consequently the culprit will have to offer a sacrifice to atone the earth goddess. Abortion is also a very serious offence in Islam and Christianity, two major religions in Nigeria. On the surface and as of now, the legalization of abortion in Nigeria is very remote. But for how long, one may ask?

Already there are a number of American "Charities" and Foundations operating in Nigeria as you read this. These Foundations exploit the ignorance and economic hardship situations of unsuspecting Nigerian women. Gradually and secretly they introduce contraception and different forms of abortion methods to these "market women". Literally they go to the open market places to educate and distribute these free contraceptives to the women without the knowledge of their husbands. They work through unscrupulous and money hungry local doctors and operatives. It is still illegal; it is still hush-hush;

but with the way the "almighty dollar" is changing hands there, it is just a matter of time before they are out in the open and everywhere not only in the cities but in the rural market places. Is someone in the Government aware of what is going on? You bet. You cannot underestimate the power of the dollar. This is a big concern.

A number of years ago, the Nigerian Conference of Catholic Bishops issued a warning to the American Charities and Foundations like Rockefeller and Ford Foundations, to name a few, not to kill, demoralize and corrupt the Nigerian women in the guise of offering medical gifts and aids. Again in their 2006 Plenary Meeting of March 6 through 8, the Catholic Conference of Nigerian Bishops once more condemned the foreign and local groups founding what they called "National Reproductive Health Institute" in Nigeria. There they go again with the American experiments that have ruined their own Nation. It has been well known that the fuel that keeps abortion in any society is **contraceptives.** It makes men and women promiscuous and insensitive to the consequences of sexual encounters. When contraceptives fail, as they often do, abortion becomes the back-up plan. Unfortunately this happens too often. Even now some Americans are not satisfied with contraceptives, or abortion, as they are. They are now choosing sterilization. Dr. Allan Rosenfield, the Dean of Columbia University School of Public Health, said that there are about 12 million couples in the United States who are protected through sterilization. In the September 25, 1990 issue of San Francisco Chronicles, a Staff writer, Peter Fimrite wrote: "Health Professionals say that without any real advances in contraception in 25 years, more couples are opting for tubal ligations or vacectomies than any other method of pregnancy prevention." These forms of permanent or reversible contraception are ranked by Dr. Felicia Stewart, co-author of "Contraceptive Technology" as the "no.1. method in the United States". Peter Fimrite reported that in an all day conference in San Francisco organized by the Planned Parenthood Society titled "New Birth Control: developing options of the future, Dr. Stewart points to a need for more research into contraceptive devices. She and other health professionals accused the Federal Government of not putting enough emphasis on contraception. Stewart decried that "only $200 - $300 millions are spent on research and development of contraceptives" while the same Government spends $21 billion a year on consequences of teenage pregnancy. The Planned Parenthood Society will not give up even when they know that they are destroying people. In desperation they will try something else.

The method employed by these Foundations in Nigeria is very subtle. They present other medical services, which help women and children and then do their dirty job in a subterranean manner. They might cleverly tell a woman that the reason she is sick is because she has many children. Then they will offer to help her to be able to have sex and not get pregnant. Apparently the Nigerian Government has not given any indication that she knows or condones what is going on. To turn a blind eye on this well orchestrated movement by the American 'Philanthropic' Charities and Companies would amount to nothing but playing the "Russian Roulette". That is far too dangerous. If this worm continues to eat very deep into an unsuspecting society, it may be difficult to eradicate later. The American moral quagmire may then repeat itself in Nigeria unless something happens now to change the trend. It takes only one of the women already indoctrinated to start the ball rolling into the Nigerian Congress or Federal Supreme Court of Nigeria. It is obvious that the same people, who planted the seed of abortion in the first place, would vigorously support and defend the woman in court with their 'almighty' dollar and personnel services. That was how Griswold v. Connecticut (challenging the Connecticut Statute prohibiting the use of contraceptives) started with two men, who had personal and financial ambition and agenda. After many attempts through the lower and Federal Appeals Courts, Griswold and Buxton won on the grounds of maintaining the "privacy" of the First Amendment. (1965). Since the Nigerian Political System is already modeled on the American System of Government it would be rather easy to do it the way the Americans did it in 1965. It was on the basis of the 1965 success, that abortion became legal in the United States on January 22, 1973, thirty three short years ago. The two doctors with the Planned Parenthood League paved the way for the legalization of abortion in the United States by introducing the contraceptives into the American society. For those Nigerians, who think it cannot happen "in our backyard", read the hand writing on the wall. Look closely at Nigerian Universities now. There is a lot of

American influence in Nigerian Universities now. In terms of sexual morality and contraceptives, there is a lot of resemblance. I "smell" something American in the Faculty. If it smells like a duck and quacks like a duck, it must be a duck. Some of the Students and Staff now may (God forbid!) be the very attorneys and judges, or legislators who will, in the next few years, argue and decide whether abortion should be legal or not in Nigeria. This is the time for Nigerians to thoroughly examine the intentions of the United States' Government Aid, her Charities and Foundations operating in Nigeria. It has happened before and may happen again.

There was a similar Campaign started in China by Rockefeller, Sr. in the fifties and sixties. It was a huge success for the Abortionists and it has spread from there to many countries in Asia, India, Latin America and Africa. When Rockefeller Sr. went to the Federal Government of the United States of America for government involvement in his Charities, a Presidential Commission was set to develop a way to control population in these countries and geographical areas mentioned above. You might ask: why does America need to listen to the crazy Economist, Malthus and his population explosion scare and doom? She did listen. Supposedly the main reason was that if there were too many people in these Countries, America would not get enough raw materials from them for her own use. Nonsense!! However, that becomes a National issue. In 1959 the Presidential Commission on population control concluded that information on contraceptives should be shipped to third world countries. But the American Roman Catholic Church had still some influence in the Administration then; the President, Dwight Eisenhower grew cold feet about the idea and the so-called aid package was scrapped. Thank God. But wait; the powerful birth control group heavily lobbied the next President, a so-called "Catholic", President John F. Gerald Kennedy and he included birth control studies in the Federally funded National Institutes of Health. That was how the Federal Family Planning started. Millionaire Rockefeller succeeded after all in getting the American Government involved in the spread and mission of contraceptives to third world countries like Nigeria. In fact, Nigerians should adopt the "Beware of the Greeks bearing gifts" attitude when dealing with the United States of America's Aid packages. The results have been devastating here at home and they will be worse in Nigeria and any other third world country, which buys into it. In reference to such gifts, "all that glitters is not gold", as the adage goes. The American Government uses tax-payer money to spread, what Pope John Paul the Second, called "the culture of death" to developing, poor and unsuspecting citizens and countries. That is immoral and unconscionable. There are groups in the United States society, which are ready to spend whatever it takes to plant the seed of "godlessness" in every country they can get into. For them it is a "religious" duty. They want to drive God as far away as they can because God gets on their conscience. They don't want God in their face or their business. They want to do what they do and still carry a straight face. But their conscience won't relieve them of the guilt. Will they succeed in Nigeria, is the question? The jury is still out on that.

For now the saving grace is that there is still a number of the "old school" in positions of power now in Nigeria. A great deal of the present politicians is the product of the Mission Schools and they still have something of the teachings they received at the back of their minds. No matter how crazy and immoral they have become, they are still afraid of going overboard. They would not sanction the legalization of abortion at this time, at least, nor would they be comfortable kicking God out of the classroom, which means kicking Him out of the Country. Even more importantly is the fact that the people of Nigeria now, Christians and Muslims alike would oppose it front, left and center. And thanks to God for that! But once more, who knows how long this situation will last? In the United States of America, it took one hundred and ninety seven years (from 1776 to 1973) to introduce abortion on demand in the land. Will it happen in Nigeria, which came into existence as an Independent Nation only in 1960? It may not happen if we do something about it now, thanks to our knowledge of the devastating effects abortion has in the United States of America and those Countries that have adopted abortion policies. Abortion in the United States of America came on the heels of the Women Liberation craze and Sexual Revolution. But if America had the kind and caliber of Americans fighting abortion and abortion laws today, America could have had a chance at saying 'no' to abortion and its proponents in 1973. Nigeria may save herself the problem of having to deal with the aftermath of abortion on women in particular and the men in their lives and society in general. Abortion makes its women woeful victims; they become desensitized and insensitive to life, and the society's value of life diminished because the one (woman) who brings life into the society is no longer interested in life. Promiscuity takes center stage in such societies. Homicides and suicides abound when the young women could no longer bear the pain, the loss, the shame and stress of abortion. They now see themselves as worthless persons, who could not safeguard the gift God gave them – the precious baby. The number of psychiatric cases jumps immensely as a result of this feeling. Prison population triples. To try to get some meaning into their lives, the people affected in most cases escape into one or more of the popular addictions of identity crisis and gay life style, illicit sex, alcohol, and drugs, all of which, may end up in "Acquired Immune Deficiency Syndrome" (AIDS). From an abortion by some, we now see a progression of negative events and peoples and attitudes, which adversely impact on society. When the center (women holding the family together) can no longer hold, things are bound to fall asunder. This creates a cycle of revolving doors that lead to nowhere. Nigeria cannot afford the headaches caused by these aberrations.

In the United States of America, things are not getting better. Teen drug use has increased 60%. One in fourteen commits suicide and one in five are depressed. People get stock in a tight corner; they can't go forward and they can't retrace their steps. Frustration is incarnated into a time bomb. The addiction is not easily shaken off once immersed in. Some rich and influential doctors, lawyers, actors and actresses are intimately wedded to drugs of all types. Like expensive brides or grooms they drain the family fortune before they become aware of what hit them. Too late, they are now homeless. Innocent young people made the wrong turn in life and lost all hope and faith in themselves, humanity, God and redemption. Many of them check out of this life without a mark to show that they passed through here. That is the way it goes with people who marry illusion, addiction, the distant cousin of 'freedom without boundaries" and "pro-abortion" philosophy. Nigeria is not ready to step into the same shoes that America is uncomfortably wearing at the moment. Nigeria hopefully has a better definition of freedom. Again this could change. But God forbid!

Relationship and cooperation between Nations are good things. One nation giving aids to another is a beautiful thing any day. But it should not be a means of coercion, misleading, intimidating or exploiting another nation. Aids to another country should not be a way to force the recipient nation to the standards of the donor nation. It will be immoral if a country says to another: "We will send you food to feed your people if you will agree to encourage the use of birth control methods in your country." That is why Nigeria should be extra careful when accepting aids from Foundations like Ford or Rockefeller and many other charities operated by American Actors and Actresses, or making business deals with the United States of American Government if such gifts and deals have immoral strings attached.

On October 31, 2003, the United States Coast Guard decommissioned CGC Sassafras, the Coast Guard's last seagoing 180-foot buoy tender, and transferred her to the Federal Republic of Nigeria as NNS Obula. The almost sixty year old ship was commissioned in 1944 and it was immediately put to good use in World War 11. In the signing over ceremony, Rear Admiral Charles Wurster, commander of the 14th District, said:

"May the Nigerian naval ship Obula (NNS Obula) serve your country as well as Sassafras has served ours."

Responding the Commanding Officer of NNS Obula, Captain Johnson Olutoyin said:

"Today is a bittersweet day. There must be a feeling of sadness in the hearts of the Sassafras crew and the people of Guam, Commonwealth of Northern Mariana Islands and the Federated States of Micronesia that your dear old Sassafras has ceased to be. On the other hand, there is a feeling of excitement in the hearts of the Nigerian crew for that another vessel has been added to the fleet of the Nigerian navy."

That was a good gesture of cooperation if that is the whole story. Nigeria should be immensely grateful to the U. S. Navy if that is the end of the story.

MARRIAGE AND DIVORCE, NIGERIAN STYLE:

Earlier we said something about the Nigerian society. How do Nigerians understand the concept of Freedom with responsibility, Freedom that has accountability? Marriage in Nigeria is and has always been between a man and a woman. In Nigeria, people do not get up one morning and declare their own rules of what marriage should be on their own. In the era before Christianity, polygamy was common. In the agrarian society more women and eventually more children were an asset on the farms to produce food. Another factor that fostered polygamy was not having a male issue to survive the man and keep the lineage going after the man had died. Having a son, who would replace a man when he dies, was a big deal in most Nigerian societies before the advent of Christianity and there are still some vestiges of that left today, Christianity notwithstanding. But it has a different face today. When a man's wife did not have any child at all or did not give him some male issues, the man was constrained by social pressure and the desire for a successor, to marry another wife in order to get some male issues, who would perpetuate his line. It was much like what King Henry V111 of England did to get a son who would be the next King of England after him. As we know that it was that mess that contributed to the birth and establishment of the Church of England and a split in the Catholic Church about five hundred years ago. Of course their knowledge of biology was very limited then to know that most of the time the fault of a couple not having a child or a male issue was from the man. But in the midst of all that, divorce was still out of the question in the Nigerian context. It is only in a very extra-ordinary circumstance that a married woman would be sent away from her matrimonial home. Invariably and ordinarily all the wives and children in a polygamous family live together as one big family with shared responsibilities. It is of course true that these polygamous families have their own fights and misunderstandings too like any monogamous family and this is not an endorsement of polygamy at all on my part. I'm simply stating the facts.

There are many kinds of models of polygamous families. The adoption of these formulas depends on the man of the house and the women, their temperaments and how they get along. Some agree with the formula, where one wife cooks for everyone in the household for a week before the other wife takes over. While one is in charge of the kitchen for that week, the other wife or wives would have other assignments of farm work, trading or any other kind of business venture, or taking care of the children or other household chores. After all these are children of one man forming brothers and sisters and half brothers and half sisters. Another formula would be for each woman to feed and take care of her own children and of course, her husband. In that case the man will eat from all the women. The first wife, who is supposedly barren, or has no son, is respected by all the wives and their children because of her seniority. Invariably the man treats her as the queen. She treats all the children as her children and they all call her "big mother" (big mama) or simply "Mother". This, in a way, follows the Old Testament model. The formula for feeding the husband also varies. In the event of the man having a misunderstanding with one of the wives, there would rarely be a divorce between him and the woman especially if she has at least a son. It should be made clear here that this writer is not an advocate of polygamy at all. Instead it is fair to say that polygamy is the better of two bad practices – polygamy and divorce. While divorce separates and tears children apart, polygamy takes care of all the children by all the parents in most part. The children of the family, though with different mothers, learn to live and cooperate with each other; they learn to tolerate and bear with one another. This situation, which they did not create, makes them strong and independent achievers. It strengthens the "Extended family System", which has been very beneficial in shaping that society. In an extended family system, the grown ups in that family group help the younger ones; the educated older ones help to educate the next generation coming up irrespective of whose children they may be because that generation of children will take up and care for the next. The system continues. It is a great system. In one sense, divorce can be equally described as a "progressive polygamy" – many wives, one at a time.

In the Christian era Nigeria, divorce is even more out of the question. Matrimony, in both traditional, Christian and Muslim religions in Nigeria, is a very strong institution. A marriage in the

Nigeria context is not just a relationship between a husband and wife especially in the Southern part; it involves all the relatives on both sides of the marriage. Hence the idea of terminating a marriage contract, wound not be an easy proposition in that society. When there is a misunderstanding between husband and wife, every effort is made through relatives, the extended family, on both sides, official witnesses of the marriage as well as the marriage sponsors and faith groups, to save the troubled marriage. Ninety five percent of the time, the marriage is saved. One of the main reasons for the success has always been the good of the children. Parents would put their differences aside and satisfy the needs of their children. Nigerian parents are less *selfish* when it comes to the good of their children. After all, marriage is a decision that adults make. A couple can always decide to give each other *another chance* to live together, to love each other and be happy with each other *again* because the union of a man and a woman in marriage is out of love and love is sacrifice, an emptying of oneself for the beloved one. The Nigerian society seems to understand the dynamics of marriage right from the beginning, even before the arrival of Christianity not only because of love but because also of the *precious fruits of the union*, the children. On the other hand, the American couple put their own interests before the interests of the children.

The idea of marriage being a decision is an old concept among the Nigerian people. It is not how you met your spouse; it is the decision you make that makes the marriage work. It is not who found your spouse initially (you directly or some one else introduced him/her to you) that makes the marriage work; it is the decision to commit yourself to your spouse at the time and continue to commit yourself, that creates a long and lasting relationship in marriage. In Nigeria many of the marriages are started through a third party. In Europe and America this process is described as "an arranged marriage", (whatever they mean by that) a terminology that is by implication derogatory. At the same time, it is not considered derogatory in America to arrange what Americans call a "blind date" for a friend or relative. It is considered appropriate for one to get a marriage partner through "on-line-dating" services, which are all over the place. To find a friend on line, or have a pen friend through a newspaper advertisement are all civilized and fine. But if an African girl recommends her girl friend to her brother, it becomes arranged marriage and uncivilized.

NIGERIA AND THE GAME THAT IS DATING:

Judging from the way Americans "date", one can safely say that there was no dating in Nigeria before Nigerians delved deeply into the life and customs of the European and American people. The point of departure may just be in the definition of the word 'dating'. That will be the reason why what is described as dating in America is not popular or wide spread in Nigeria. When one talks about "dating" in America, it is to a certain degree more of "having fun" and less of looking for a life partner. Ordinarily in Nigeria, it is the other way round. When a man was ready to get married, he would go straight to making a serious and genuine search for a wife. He could tell his friends and relatives, especially his sisters, to help him find a suitable wife. These people, who really know him, his character and temperament, would use them as a kind of measurement to look for a life partner for him. They would each have an idea of a good match for him. He would also give them an idea of the external description, and profession of the lady he would like to live with the rest of his life. Of course the most important of all would be her character, not external beauty. Family background and her belief system would be very high because these would be the most likely things to start problems later. The family background on both sides is very important. There is an old advice sometimes given to a man, who is looking for a spouse: "Carefully look at and study your mother in-law to-be, before you say 'I do'." That makes sense because 90% of the time, the daughter acts and behaves like her Mom and looks like her in old age. If he knows what to expect before saying "I do", he can cope with any outcome better because it is his decision after all, if he chooses to go on with the wedding. This careful scrutiny is there because the people believe that marriage is *for ever* "till death do us part", not a casual encounter. There is no condition placed on the marriage. That is also the foundational reason why divorce is not a normal route in a troubled marriage in the Nigerian system. If Americans put in a little more effort in selecting a life partner, there would be no need to have 50% of American marriages end up in divorces.

When this man finds a girl or one is introduced to him by a friend or family, both he and the girl would then get to know each other for some time. This is the only place that one can squeeze in the word 'dating' in the Nigerian context. The studying is for the couple as well as their families. If he is satisfied with the girl and the girl feels the same way about him, the man would officially introduce himself to her family and declare his intention of marriage to her parents. Since, invariably her family would not know enough about the prospective husband and his family, neither her nor her family would give any answer to this proposal until they had made some inquiry and background check regarding him and his family. The family of the girl would like to know how the men in that family treat their wives; if they have any serious genetic disease; if the members of his family get along with other families in the village or place etc.

Assuming that everything in the inquiry was positive, the family of the girl would officially invite the man and his family to come for an answer to the official marriage proposal. But before then the man's family would take time to make inquiries about the lady and her family because marriage is a serious business, which is for life. Marriage was never for trial as in many cases in the United States especially Hollywood; it was real and it was final. If people wanted their marriage to be successful and final, they would invest time and energy into it. Eventually there would be a ceremony where the girl would officially accept his hands in marriage publicly in a traditional way. We won't go into details. If they are all pagans, the new couple would receive blessings from their parents and perhaps, their chief priest. They are now declared husband and wife. To arrive at this stage takes some time, anywhere from months to a year and sometimes years. Apart from the ceremonies, and financial expenditures involved, time is used to solidify the relationship. But if they are Christians, they were not allowed to live together until they have been married in the Church. After the pagan or Christian wedding, the two families and in fact the two villages, where each spouse comes from, shall have entered a pact of love and friendship, which cannot be broken easily just by the two original people, who brought them together in the first place. In those days of inter-tribal wars, the matrimonial pact between two villages could prevent a war. It is on that pact that this marriage draws strength, in good times and bad. This kind of strong family tie helps the Nigerian society to avoid divorce. And it is worth the wait. The American teen falling "in love" is not realistic because they are not capable of a commitment as serious as marriage. That is why such marriages never last when they settle down to find out that they have no business getting together in the first place; that marriage is a whole lot more than sleeping together; that falling in love really means a willingness to carry each other's burden. In the Nigerian formula, the man knows that he has to attain a certain matured age, have a certain amount of education or skills and property to support a family. There is a marked difference between the young Nigerian boy and girl and a young American boy and girl in their attitude toward marriage. While the Nigerian looks forward to building a family of father, mother and children, the American looks forward to building a relationship of husband and wife. But experience has shown that the couple alone relationship is illusive and does not work because it is not natural. It is a perfect recipe for divorce because it feeds on ego and selfishness and competing interests. Couples exist to form families of husbands, wives and children, the effect and fruit of the union. It becomes complete like the Trinitarian Father, Son and Holy Spirit.

But there is a genuine concern now about the American influence on Nigerian marriages of tomorrow. Since everything from America is held in very high esteem in Nigeria, divorce may enjoy such approbation in years to come. In fact it has even started with some Nigerians in the U. S. already getting divorce in America. They think they are bringing "Freedom" home to Nigeria. Poor fellows!! That will have devastating effect, not just on the Nigerian soil, but on the African Continent because of the special place Nigeria enjoys in Africa. Such a move would unleash moral decadence and sexual promiscuity in Nigeria. The already sufficiently saturated ills of other kinds in the Nigerian society will multiply tenfold. The Mexican experience would be "a piece of cake" compared to what could happen in Nigeria if the trend is not reversed soon. Close proximity to the United States of America has its freebees and liabilities too. Mexico, where the girls used to be morally decent, has now become a sexually charged and liberated Nation and their young men have taken to drugs, alcohol and violence in the United States, on the boarders and in Mexico itself. Guns and drug trafficking, gay-life style, and gang culture are gradually becoming normal among Mexicans in Mexico and America. Some young boys come across the boarder to make money as sex slave. Scenes from Mexican television stations in the U. S. are too sexually explicit. If America is let in one way or the other into a country, the so-called American Freedom will rub off on that country. America's long association with the Philippines has had the same results. It is a very funny combination when a third world country buys into the luxury, pleasures, and free-life styles of America and don't have what it takes to realize or maintain them. It is phony and awkward. A simple and happy people suddenly see themselves stretching for what they can't legally reach. They see a small fraction in their population living large and they are sucked into the temptation of greed and get-rich-quick desire. The resultant dissatisfaction and depression lead to frustration, sex addiction, drugs and violence. It will never work out that a nation like Nigeria survive the cultural shock of that magnitude after a cultural encounter with a nation like America. The Bible aptly described it thus in Mark's Gospel, Chapter 2: verse 21: "No one patches old clothes by sewing on a piece of new cloth. The new piece would shrink and tear a bigger hole." When poor countries like the Philippines, Mexico and Nigeria try to live the American way of life, they run the risk of ending worse than they started. As big and rich as America is, she has not been able to shake off the mess dumped on her since the sexual revolution of the sixties. Instead of getting better, she is getting worse.

We have tried to show that freedom, American style, is not real freedom and Nigeria should not even touch that kind of freedom with "a ten foot pole". The unfortunate thing is that Nigerians know how to copy and perfect bad behaviors. Of late Nigerian boys and men have started to pierce their ears and wear ear-rings, bread and color their hairs like some American men. Some have also started to plait their hairs like some black Americans for no meaningful reason except that some rich Actors, Basket ball, Football and Base ball players do that. It is almost like they have a euphoric sense that they will be as rich as the Actors, Football and Base ball stars, if they dress like them. The very, very small number of young men doing this also know that they will be looked upon as girls or women at home if they wear ear-rings or plait or color their hair. These could only bring them shame and isolation in Nigeria because men in that society don't try to look like women. It is like one escaping into drugs, sex or alcohol to run away from some trouble only to wake up to see that nothing has changed. When these Nigerian boys adopt these fashion displays like Nigerian girls, they look out of play among their own people. There are many things to learn from America; freedom isn't one of them. It is essential that the traditions and customs of marriage be maintained in the Nigerian society because they have warded off irresponsible marriage unions, which would have ended in divorces.

Unlike the American society, where couples like to be the same age, the Nigerian men should continue to be older than their wives by about seven to ten years. One of the factors that contribute to divorce in America is the fact that two twenty year old "hot-heads", who have a marriage problem, have no way or experience of life to step back and think dispassionately about their present problems in order to solve them without divorce. Here we have two people, who have no skills yet to handle marriage. But if the man were older and more mature, chances are that he would rise above the issue in order to resolve it. Unlike Nigerians, many Americans marry young, and do everything in their power to exclude their parents in the marriage proposals and arrangements. Even in America, those ethnic groups, which involve their parents and family members in the marriage proposals from the onset, have fewer divorces than those ethnic groups, which don't.

The Institution of marriage in Nigeria has a more solid base than in America. As was hinted above, there is a certain maturity in a man that is essential to start a family. A man is expected to have some basic things for a household in order to be ready to start a family of his own. Shelter and land ownership are key components to his readiness to bring a woman home. To accomplish this he must have finished school or has gone through some kind of trade, which would insure him a good job. Then he would start to think about getting married. In America, people start with "a person" before looking for the means to make it happen. The ego gets in the way. The only thing wrong with this is that, more often than not, the attachment to "the person" is mere infatuation not love. A good number of marriages have such beginnings and they crash at the first impact, like a minor disagreement in the house. In the Nigerian experience, the age difference gives the two people enough time to get ready for marriage. Nothing is left to chance because it is supposed to be a one time, sacred duty unless death intervenes. It is only when the man is ready that he makes a move toward establishing a family since marriage is a decision. His readiness includes having enough money to pay the bride price. Some people might frown at this noble custom; but it is a wise one. It shows a certain degree of maturity in a man. The man's willingness to go through these customary preparations and upheavals is a testimony that the lady is worth fighting for and must be really what his heart wants. It is a worthwhile sacrifice for the one he loves. Now we are talking about love in the true sense – what one gives and not what one receives. This may be foreign to an American audience of today; but it is one of the strong pillars of the foundation of marriage in most parts of Nigeria. It can be a rigorous experience, but it is worth it. There are some other cultures that subject a man to all kinds of strenuous feats to win the love of a girl. In some cultures a man has to prove his love by facing an opposing suitor in a duel. Let us flash back to the Old Testament. To marry his wife, Rachel, Jacob had to work for his father in-law for seven years. When he was tricked by his father in-law and Uncle Laban, to marry Leah, the older daughter instead of her sister Rachel, whom Jacob really loved, he had to work for another seven years to finally marry his choice. He ended up marrying the two sisters. That is a custom that tests the strength, determination and caliber of a man seeking to get married. If Nigeria loses this custom through association with America, one of the foundational pillars of marriage in Nigeria shall have been lost. For those Nigerians in the United States of America, the battle is not completely lost. So far many young Nigerian men, who live in the United States are still heeding to this custom when they go to Nigeria to choose a wife. But how long will this good custom last? Good question! Who knows? While their fathers go to Nigeria to subject themselves to the custom to marry their mothers, the children born here in the United States by Nigerian parents, are not heeding to that custom. That creates some concern about the future of this custom for Nigerians in America. But one thing is clear; it has contributed a great deal to check divorce and Nigerian children are the beneficiaries of a non-divorce society.

MY NIGERIAN BROTHERS' KEEPER:

My brother's keeper concept is as old as mankind itself. When we see harm coming the way of our brother, we warn him to avoid such a harm because we love our brother. Scripture tells us to watch one another's back. If we hit a big "sale", we get on the phone immediately to tell our brothers and sisters to come on down. In that famous passage in the Bible, when God asked Cain, about his brother Abel, whom he had killed, (perhaps the first fratricide), Cain replied: "who has made me my brother's keeper?" Cain was trying, in vain, to hide his heinous action of killing his brother. I hope we will not ask God the same question. As Americans we are losing the sense of our brother's keeper concept by the day in a lot of areas of our lives. In the forties and fifties, it was alive and well across America. The next door-neighbor's son or daughter was your son or daughter. You could give them a ride home from school or the mall. But not anymore for various and obvious reasons! Then your neighbor could discipline your kids on the street, without reference to you, if your kids misbehaved. That neighbor would come to your house to tell you what the kids did and how he punished them, unless the kids were smart enough to make a deal with you not to tell their parents because they were sure to get another punishment from their parents, if they knew. That was a life time lesson for the kids. At that period kids were cautious not to get into mischief because the whole neighborhood was their home and every body in the neighborhood was their parent or keeper. Everybody watched everybody's back. Yes, you were your brother's keeper. One did not know when and where one of many parents would pop up from. Young people could honestly say that the parents of their friends were their parents and the parents could honestly say that the friends of their children were their children also. That made the neighborhood one big family where everybody becomes a brother's keeper. Children had little or no distractions. There was no need for rival gangs. They did their home-work and went out to play without any parent overly worried about the whereabouts of their children. Kidnapping was a word that existed pretty much in the dictionary only. That was then; this is now. That scenario could have been Nigeria or America in the thirties, forties or the fifties. Today there are kidnappings of children everyday across America. Parents are now constantly in a stress mode because nobody wants to go through the ordeal of having their child kidnapped, molested or even murdered. Before the First Amendment was misrepresented, it was a pleasure having and raising children and many of them for that matter. People loved children and were only too happy to get involved in raising them.

But all that went to the drains with the arrival of the sixties, when social morality came under serious attacks. The sixties' revolution divided people, and atheistic psychologists put undue and misplaced emphasis on individualism and personal rights, sex and freedom; they demonized punishment by calling it abuse; and created the god of relativism. These psychologists introduced the idea that no action is good or bad. Everything depended on each individual to decide. Therefore to let the children loose to do whatever they want, was their way to train our children. That was how America started to lose the family and children and the brotherhood. Of course if there was no right or wrong, there would be no room anymore in the neighborhood to control the kids and no need for parents to show good example to their children. With that mirror presented to the children, there were no more inhibitions. For some educators in the school system, inhibition is a word that should not be mentioned to children because they say that inhibition is an enemy to "freedom" and personality growth. Thus we moved from a society where it took a "whole village to raise a child" to one where one could not even manage his own children let alone try to help the children of the village or neighborhood without being attacked and insulted by the parents of those children. A parent is no longer at liberty to train his/her children without the threat of the children calling the police on the parent. Everybody's hands are now tied to give developing children the real lessons of life. Instead all that the policy makers want the children to know is that they are "Americans and free". They have Constitutional rights to *do* and *say* whatever they want under the guarantees of the First Amendment. This becomes the beginning of youth problems in society: talking back to neighbors and parents; cutting school; under age smoking, drinking, burglary and all kinds of dangerous drugs, until some end up in prison or have their own children, who will end up in prison too. Ironically it is the same Mr. Policy Maker, who will put these "free American kids" in prison. Smart policy, you would say? What a difference a couple of years make in the way America raised her children and played "brother's keeper" and now!

The concept of being our brother's keeper has always been a part of the Nigerian society. It is an off shoot of the "Extended Family" system in Nigeria. The strength of the family is the basis of the strength of the extended family system. Europe and America lost the extended family system when the very nucleus of society was fractured through contraceptives, abortion and divorce. In Europe and America then, families would send their son or daughter to be raised by a grand mother, an uncle or aunt. That was part of the extended family structure. In Nigeria the average family has five or six children. In the United States of America the average number of children per family is about 1.7. When you are one of five siblings, you learn and understand love and suffering fast. You are more likely to appreciate one another better. Sharing and struggling are learned and practiced intensely in the family where there are five children or more. The instinct of survival is sharpened in this kind of a family. The reality of God's presence and providence is very clearly defined. The generosity of giving oneself to the service of God in a religious vocation becomes a little easier both for the individual and the family. Those characteristics are the essential ingredients of family, nucleus or extended, from which Brother's keeper concept is derived. The strong family ties, the extended family system are the bedrock of the Nigerian society. That has always kept the momentum of progress going. Big brother helps to train his brother or sister in school. Years down the road, big brother is no longer financially strong; then small brother or sister takes up the training of big brother's sons or daughters and that cycle continues. Excellent tradition and culture! But this too can change and in fact is beginning to change because of the Nigerian association with the West, especially in America, where individualism is very strong. Immediately some of these Nigerians in the U. S. get married, there seems to be a dichotomy between the original family in Nigeria and the new one in America. Some of the new wives begin to think Western or American namely: 'this marriage is between just the two of us.' That statement alone begins to eat into the long tested extended family system. It begins to fracture and break not just the big extended Nigerian family but the nucleus family just started. Some of the married Nigerian women cultivate the "gold digger" mentality of some American women; all they want is divorce in order to take the big house and be independent of a man. This is a very dangerous trend that must be checked. Thank God it is just a few Nigerians that are yet involved in this. The sense of aloofness in the face of family business or problem is very un-Nigerian. But unconsciously some Nigerians with an American influence or connection have started to look at aloofness the gentlemanly way to be. "Mind your own business" is gradually becoming golden. Casual visit to a friend or relative without prior invitation is in the verge of being called uncivil by these "new Nigerians". Social relationships between family and friends are being reduced to business relationships of "what can I do for you"? This is not the Nigerian way. Though in a very minimal way, this trend of losing the sense of "my brother's keeper concept" is real. That is why Nigerian association with the United States of America should be under constant surveillance. To a certain extent, this generation of Nigerians, have no appreciation of what a nice heritage they have in these age tested cultural values.

Earlier we talked about the influence American educational system has on Nigerian education and the raising of children. Though there is still a fairly amount of discipline in Nigerian schools, something in discipline has been lost too. Left to the Government alone, there would be no need of discipline in school at all. These, as we said before, are American-trained or those who were trained by American-trained Professors and Lecturers in Nigerian universities. And there are many of them in Nigeria today. They want to transfer American education into Nigeria without any editing. On the tertiary level, this American trend has caught on. But it has not made its way completely to the grade school level, while the high school level has some infiltrations already. Insubordination, cutting school, cigarette smoking and sex are being reported in a very small number of High Schools. Without the cooperation of "Parents Teachers Associations" and "Board of Governors" in the running of these schools, it could have spread even faster. Of course there is a slight difference between the way these negative behaviors affect students in the city schools and those in the rural areas, between those in one part of the Country and another. There are still some parts of the Country where any adult man regards himself as the 'father' of all the children in the village and any woman regards all the children in the village as her 'children'. If there is any reason to discipline any child, it is done without reference to the actual or blood father or mother. The success of any child in the place is the success and glory of all, while the failure of one child in the area is the failure of all. It is interesting that religious schools and private schools are run differently. There is absolute discipline. The result is that students in these religious and private schools have the best results in the nation. It is ironic too that it is in these religious schools that the Government officials send their own children. Go figure that.

CHAPTER SIX:
SHAME, EGO, LUST AND RAPE

When we talk about shame, the general connotation in America is something which is undesirable and negative. Is shame synonymous with negativity? No! Shame is an emotion which shows remorse or regret for falling short of an expected standard of behavior or performance. According to Webster dictionary, shame is described as a painful emotion caused by consciousness of guilt, short-coming, or impropriety. In another sense it is something that brings censure or reproach or something to be regretted. Now let's work with that definition. According to the foregoing when a human being does some acts, which bring censure or reproach on the individual or another, that individual or another feels ashamed of the acts. That is a good thing. It causes regrets or at least should. It arouses guilt-feelings in the individual, who performed the action or others, who saw the action. The consciousness of this impropriety is the beginning of the individual's recovery or redemption if well handled. In religious circles it is called "repentance". Without this awareness, there could not be repentance or redress.

IS THERE ANYTHING GOOD IN SHAME?:

Very recently in the history of American, something went wrong vis a vis shame. It became "politically incorrect" to be ashamed of an impropriety. No wonder people do all kinds of things. Unfortunately this societal change in attitude came from the Behavioral Sciences.

Children and then adults were taught that shame acts as an inhibition to the wholeness or full development of an individual. This trend turns out to be what Shakespeare called "a stamp of one defect", which will eventually play a negative role in all future actions of a lot of people and may cause their downfall. When you remove the sense of shame from an individual, he becomes capable of doing "anything" at all without any qualms, I mean anything from the gross to the absurd without any feeling of remorse. Some go as far as becoming perverts because someone removed the sense of shame from them. Such people can set their neighbor's house on fire and stand at the corner and enjoy the blaze. They could rape their sisters or close relatives and laugh at it. And if one such person's crying sister threatened to tell their parents, he would say: "Tell them; I don't care." In the evening he would sit on the opposite side of the dinner table and shamelessly eat with his sister, whom he raped. This young, shameless boy set for disaster, would eventually grow up to sleep with his fourteen year old daughter and tell her that he was expressing his love for her. "Don't tell anyone; this is our little secret," he would say. This pervert would expose himself before his daughter and any young girl that comes his way and have no qualms of conscience. There is a growing number of people like that in our society today as we condone the absence of shame in our society. These people, men and women and young adults, would stand in front of the camera and use foul language, dance dirty, pose nude on front pages of newspapers and magazines without minding the parents or family members seeing or watching them on television. They call it free speech and First Amendment rights. Some parents in this category would describe their nude daughter as very cute and sexy. It would not be any big deal for these kinds of individuals to go on Television Talk Shows to discuss how they cheat on their spouses or make money selling their bodies and receive great applause from the audience. Such audiences are equally stupid because they have no shame either. There have been many cases of young women, who would not feel any shame coming on Television for a DNA test to find out who is the biological father of their babies. On finding out that it is not boy-friend "A", the shameless girls would say it must be boy-friend "B" etc. One of these girls on this particular Murray Povich Show presented boy-friends she had sex with up to the seventh man in an effort to find the father of her baby and the DNA result was still negative for each of them. She slept with so many men that she could not know who the exact father of her baby was. This was happening on National Television for everybody to see. There could be many such women out there. But shamelessly coming on National Television is a whole other matter. Some people in the audience cheered for her and some hooted her down. Where is the shame and where is the model for young girls to follow? There was no shame. If there was any shame left in her, she would not have done what she did. Secondly, after she had done a shameful thing, she would not have paraded herself on National Television showing bad example to other women. But on the other hand, she was doing only what she has been taught and conditioned to do by Psychologists – not to be ashamed.

Of course the same thing goes on among our University student on campus and elsewhere. There is no shame at all among College students, who every year go on "Spring Break" to Holiday Resorts just to get wild, expose themselves to thousands of fellow students and millions of people watching the National Television including their parents, brothers and sisters. They get drunk, have multiple sex partners and act stupid. There is no national outrage at all.

Who is talking about shame when some single Moms try to steal their daughters' boy-friends? They fight over them, and expose themselves and face off on Jerry Spinger or Maury Povich Television Talk Shows without any shame whatsoever. Where did decency go? One of the Moms on the Show claimed to give her daughter's boy-fried a better satisfaction than her daughter could give him. Who is ashamed when a man and his son finished smoking dope together and go to share a whore in the house? Where is our shame when a woman, with a teenage son and a teenage daughter in her house, would bring her thirteen year old student and boy-friend in the house and have sex with him? She went to prison for it, had a child for him while in prison, divorced her husband and married her boy lover after doing time. Shamelessly they went from one Television station to another telling their "shameful" story. Who is complaining about a divorced single Mom, who lets her teenage daughter and her teenage boyfriend have sex in her home with her permission even when she is home? When she was asked why she let that practice go on in her house, she said on Television that it was better for her that her daughter is having sex in her house than somewhere she doesn't know. There is no public outcry about these shameful behaviors, which are slowly becoming ordinary in our society. Any surprise that things are the way they are? It is the sign of freedom.

How did people turn this way, you may ask? It was a seed planted long time ago by parents, psychologists, teachers, legislators, and I say, society. It started when we as a nation, abandoned the old way and started calling a sense of shame a bad name even when someone acts shamefully. It happened when we declared ourselves free of conscience. It happened when we chose to disown the word shame by doing shameful things and feel good doing them. It happened when Americans, or at least their representatives, said that freedom is a license to do and say anything in the name of the First Amendment. Some people saw it coming and spoke up but nobody was listening. Now the cat is out of the bag. She has grown wild and it is very difficult to put her back into the bag. Added to the non-shame is the fact that women are the ones, who are being exploited. Women left themselves to be used and abused as toys and playthings to be displayed on bookstands on stores and markets. It is degrading to womanhood. One would think that women would, with one voice, condemn this shameful exploitation of women by the highest bidder. But that does not happen. It is the women who appear naked or half naked on hundreds of magazines on display throughout the markets in the United States and abroad. Feminist Groups and other Women Organizations like National Organization of Women (NOW) promote these abuse and misuse of womanhood as an empowerment of women. Some people in general complain about the perversion but feel powerless about doing something about it. Those who can do something about it in Congress are either perverted themselves or are afraid of powerful interest groups, who pay for their re-election campaigns. There are people who make money off these anomalies. After all Hollywood makes her money by permissiveness and nudity; the more body the ladies show the higher position and more money and important roles they get in the industry. If an Actress is not willing to go "down and dirty" as the saying goes, she will not go beyond a supporting role. If you want to know what Hollywood is about, watch the Emmys, the Oscars and other Awards. It is not only a show of jewelry; it is a show of body parts for the Actresses. It is almost like a competition of who would reveal more and still have a little something on. Talking about shame, this is of course, on National TV and their children are watching too. The pass word is "to be cute and sexy" and America is watching and the rates go up.

There are nude colonies in parts of America. They say it is freedom of expression. A time is coming, and in fact, it is almost here, when these colonies will gain their "right" and "freedom" of association with the rest of the nation. Why should they be segregated? That is against the First Amendment. The gays and lesbians have done it. The Nudist Colonies would claim their "rights" like everyone else, to the First Amendment. They would stage some Rallies and a couple of Nude Pride Parades, with cameras on, be arrested and take their case to the Supreme Court. Why would they not win? Others have won. Then it would be ordinary to see people wandering in the city completely naked. No shame at all! Then we shall have landed and the American dream realized. Would people in the early nineteen hundreds believe that men and women, and teens go to the City Park full of people in the day light and engage in passionate kisses that sometimes end up in intercourse and people are passing by? Instead of them getting ashamed, you get ashamed of seeing them. Would our forefathers believe that men are now married to men and women married to women, all legal? What manner of shame would you think was hovering over at Woodstock village when there was free sex, free drugs, free for all? Yet a group of people could not gather in the same City Park and pray or sing religious songs. A rapper cursing and full of profanity would be allowed to sing. But no religious songs! These shameless people are permitted to play loud music with indecent lyrics while the Cross or any religious object would not be allowed on the ground. Groups like ACLU would say that people who did not like the lyrics could leave the Park or if on T.V. they should turn it off. But people who do not like religious songs and objects could not be asked to leave if they don't like religious songs or objects in a public place. Shamelessness and indecency have won over prayer on a public ground. Shame!

So is shame a good or bad thing? In any way you look it, and no matter how you slice it, human beings need to act reasonably in order to continue to be human beings the way God intended. Does anyone expect animals to feel a sense of shame? They don't feel shame because they do not have conscience and cannot reason. Shame is what happens when a person, through deductive reasoning, discovers some incongruity in his behavior. That is to say that he sees in his action, or sometimes in somebody else's action, something very much below an action expected of a human being. The action falls short of human expectation. The natural consequence is what rationality calls shame, shame for oneself or for other people's actions. Animals don't share this kind of rationality with us. That is why animals don't distinguish between mother or father, brother or sister when it is their mating season. The only distinction made is male or female. Every other animal of the same species and different sex is fair game. Yes, that is what happens in the animal world. The line of demarcation is getting thin and blurred between us and them. Ours is a human world. When shame is removed from human beings by choice or some times through mental incapacity (madness or under the influence of drugs or alcohol), they begin to act like animals. That is why crazy people do not care about how they dress or appear. The Hippies of the sixties are a good example of what we are talking about. That era ushered in the drug culture and the sexual revolution that is our headache today. I think it is fair to say that if you do not have the sense of shame, you will likely do any crime on the books. It is in this state of mind that a man can lose respect for his daughter, sister, maid or any woman, for that matter. In this frame of purely animal mind, every female becomes fair game for him, because he is operating more on the animal level than the human level. Why do we have an increased number of cases of rapes today? Like an animal, a rapist has to satisfy the sexual appetite *now* without any reference to reason. Reason has disappeared and society has fully endorsed it in principle. This is the reason we have an increase of cases of abominations of incest and general disrespect for women in our society now by men. In the same token we have an increase of ladies disrespecting, abusing and devaluing themselves today than ever before. They say it is women freedom and liberation. These increases were unheard of some years ago.

In recent years we have tried to prosecute some cases of rape and incest. But we forget that we as a society contributed to their behavior by putting in place destabilizing factors one of which is the removal of shame in society. We programmed people to grow up without having a sense of shame or even respect for people. Now they act dishonorably and shamelessly because there is no shame in their eyes and the law is after them. The prosecution of these people will not bring back sanity in that area of society's life. There has to be re-education of people starting with today's young people. Hopefully the next generation of people will pick it up. As for many people in this generation, it is over. "Call the next case."

The present governments and legislators have to be courageous to put laws in place to fashion a brighter future for our kids and the next generation. They need to let people know that there are some actions that we should be ashamed of. It is a responsibility incumbent on them to let folks understand that human and individual freedom has some limitations. There should be a clearer reading of the First Amendment by Congress. Trial Attorneys and excessively liberal Judges should be checked by Congress. While one may have the freedom to be naked in his or her room, he or she does not have the freedom to walk naked on the street because there are other individuals, who have the freedom to enjoy the same street without seeing naked people. Right there is a limitation on ones freedom to go naked. Until Congress takes such steps, it is unfair even to prosecute anybody for these perverted offences when society helped to make them like that.

The current trend is not going to get better unless something changes. Rather it is going to get worse because we, as a nation, are justifying it and selling it abroad. Unfortunately Nigeria is one of the many nations in the world that this commodity is being sold to. Historically Nigerians have a very strong sense of the Sacred. There are a lot of social taboos, which, in the light of these events, have served as real buffers to these infiltrating cultures from the West. Sometimes Americans and people from the West think that these taboos are fetish and excessive. But without the intensity of the role these taboos and the sense of shame play in Nigeria, she would have had the same problems, conflicts and crises that are being faced in America at the present time as a result of lack of shame in their society. Respect is still part of the Nigerian culture. Before an individual, teen or adult goes off into one of those unorthodox and shameful behaviors, he/she would first think about the impact it would have on his parents and family members. After exposing her body in a shameful manner on Television, with what eyes would she go to look on her parents and family? When she thinks for a second and finds out how much reproach and embarrassment this Television appearance would bring on the *family*, she would quickly scraped the idea from her head. This is rationality in action to stop a bad or corrupt behavior. Would an American boy or girl reason like that? He or she would not be free and independent.

In the Nigerian society today, the idea of having a relative in prison is still very shameful and embarrassing to family members. But in America, it is no big deal for the same reason discussed above. In American prisons, inmates receive visitors regularly. In California it used to be four days a week. Now because of budget constraints, it is twice a week plus public holidays. In Nigeria, there is very restricted visitation for inmates. Even when it is possible to visit, family members of the incarcerated in Nigeria would not visit because of the shame and the let-down surrounding one going to prison. That makes being in prison very difficult and uncomfortable for Nigerian Inmates. But the benefit is that Nigeria has a small number of incarcerated persons. When one goes through that experience once, he would not want to go a second and third time. There is scarcely any need for "the three strikes and you are out law" as we have in California. Nigerians are not Angels by any means, when it comes to felony. By no means! But the issue at stake here is that people are not proud of coming to prison as one seems to get the impression in the United States prisons. It is rather humiliating for Nigerian Inmates. Nigerian Inmates in say, a Californian prison would not like to get anywhere close to a worker originally from Nigeria for the same reason. He or she would be ashamed to explain how he or she came all the way from Nigeria to for further his/her studies and end up in prison. But an American Inmate would almost proudly talk about his Mom in that prison while his Dad and two of his siblings are in the other prison. Some almost give the impression that they wear it as a badge of honor. This uncomfortable position, for Nigerians, makes it difficult for ex- felons to get into the habit of making prison a vacation spot with a revolving door.

Just a few years ago, Nigeria refused to host the World Beauty Pageant because the image of half naked women on National Television would have been considered an embarrassment for the citizens of Nigeria at that time. The Federal Government was quite aware of the millions of dollars, which Nigeria would have made by hosting the Pageant. But she gave it up for a greater good. It boils down to what is the country's priority even though one of the Pageants was a Nigerian? To collect a few hundred millions of dollars now in revenue and spend a couple of billions of dollars to do damage control a few years later!

Fear is another word that comes to mind when discussing shame. Psychologists equally tend to give that word a bad rap. In actual fact it is good and is needed in human societies. Fear is related to respect and shame. Anyone who does not fear somebody is likely not going to have any shame in him or her. There is a respectful and filial fear in not going naked on the screen for family honor and respect. Scripture tell us that the fear of the Lord is the beginning of wisdom. Ultimately respect, fear and shame have their origin from God, who gives us conscience and reason to distinguish between good and bad, un-shameful and shameful acts. When Adam and Eve disobeyed God, they were ashamed to appear before God. That is why, for Nigerians, adherence and respect for the sacred, is a sacred duty. Even though these negative influences are around the corner, Nigerians can, with determination, hold on to the cultures and sacred institutions of the past.

WHEN IS EGO DANGEROUS?:

Ego is the indulging and seeking of the self. An ego-centric individual is one who cannot look at an issue objectively. He always sees things from his point of view. He is said to be self-centered. There is no objective truth because he cannot handle the truth especially when it is not favorable to him. In any given situation, the Ego thinks he has to defend the self even when that position is indefensible. That is one of the problems with ego-centric persons. They cannot be objective. That is to say they cannot reason well or argue well. If you are not on their side, they become angry with you. When ones philosophy is standing on the foundations of the ego, that philosophy becomes suspect and unreliable because, as an objective instrument, it cannot render objective truth or verdict.

In a general sense, the word Ego is not bad because everyone has and should have a certain degree of ego feeling of self. This is healthy because "Charity begins at home", but should not end there. If one does not love oneself one might not be able to love other people. Again self-consciousness is not a bad thing because through it, one can discover the truth about oneself and make some adjustments of ones position toward the truth. It is when it gets to the point of obsession that it begins to become a problem and an obstruction. Psychology is the study that is tasked with balancing in each individual the sense of what is healthy in the role that ego plays in a person and what is not healthy. But in the recent memory the role played by Psychology has been skewed in many countries. Some European and American Psychologists have over stepped the comfortable boundaries of psychology in this area. They have succeeded in making people so egocentric that they can no longer handle normal, developmental loss or failure in life. They have made many people so fragile that they cannot handle even small disappointments that have healthy, teaching lessons of life.

What is the one single factor that contributes to most of the problems, which stem from this egocentric but fragile attitude of a number of Americans today? It is low self esteem. Low self-esteem is like cancer that spreads and kills. When it starts, it links up with everything on its track and it is passed on from generation to generation. It is closely associated with and in many cases is the cause of addiction in the following areas of vice: drugs, smoking, alcohol, sex, prostitution, suicide, depression, divorce and school drop-out. In trying to give people high self esteem (boosting the ego), the said Psychologists have created a worse problem than they started with. This body of knowledge is being transmitted eventually to the society through the school system. Let me reiterate that some ego and self esteem are good and necessary. Like the First Amendment, it is the way they are given and applied that changes the equation.

Psychologists and a lot of people in our society think that getting someone upset is always bad. That is not true. How can one go through life without being upset or upsetting somebody when they do something wrong? Every healthy life has growing pains. Without being upset at the appropriate times, how can one learn? When a baby is born from a sheltered and comfortable womb into this harsh world, he utters a shrill cry. The 'shrill cry' is not comfortable but that is the first sign of life in this baby for the doctor, nurses and parents. It is a cry but a good and happy one. If the baby is born and he or she doesn't cry, there is a problem and the doctor or midwife will make him cry because nobody likes a still-born baby. In that example 'crying' is what confirms that there is life; this brings joy to the mother, the doctor and nurses around. It is like a necessary evil. For those who believe in Scriptures, it has backing and foundation in the Bible. The Old Testament tells us after the Fall of Adam and Eve that they will have to go through difficult times to succeed in life. That was passed on to all, who descended from Adam and Eve – us.

"To the woman he said: 'I will intensify the pangs of your childbearing; in pain shall you bring forth children. Yet your urge shall be for your husband, and he shall be your master.'

To the man he said: 'because you listened to your wife and ate from the tree of which I had forbidden you to eat, cursed be the ground because of you! In toil shall you eat its yield all the days of your life. Thorns and thistles shall it bring forth to you, as you eat of the plants of the field. By the sweat of your face shall you get bread to eat, until you return to the ground from which you were taken; for you are dirt, and to dirt you shall return.'"
Genesis: 3: 16-19. (NAB)

In the New Testament Jesus restated the same idea when He said:
"Whoever wishes to come after me must deny himself, take up his cross, and follow me. For whoever wishes to save his life will lose it, but whoever loses his life for my sake will find it." Matthew 16: 24-25.(NAB)

Yes, there will be discomfort, upset, disappointments in life. It has been like that and will continue to be like that after we have all checked out of this stage. Governments, parents and educators should have to teach our children about these downs and how to live with them. We have a glorious and teaching opportunity to train our children to be strong to withstand all the challenges that life will eventually throw at us. What kind of educational system is there, where nobody fails in the class even when everybody knows that there are some students, who do not measure up to the expected standard? This is the product of the psychologists, who say that children should not become upset, disappointed or feel a sense of shame. In order not to upset the student or the parents, every student is promoted to the next class, year after year to make everyone happy. In the classroom, the teacher cannot tell a student that the answer he gave was wrong because "that could scar the student for ever", Psychologists would say. So to make everyone happy, there is no right and no wrong answers. While it is "politically correct", it hurts the "standard", the student and the society footing the bill. It is a waste of money when a student does not know what he is said to have learned. How is such a student/graduate going to function in the real world, where practically everyone is from Missouri, the 'show me' State? There will be no Mom or Dad to threaten the teacher, no teacher to acquiesce to what everybody wants in order to pay his rent and feed his/her own family, and there will be no big brother Psychologist to defend the theory. For a lot of new graduates in the cage, failure is written all over the place. Depression may set in with all its family members: drinking, drug, sex, suicidal tendencies and all the attendant crimes to maintain the habits. In many cases there is no competitive spirit since that could make someone look inferior or even feel bad if they don't succeed. Further more, the over all "liberal education" approach is intellectually dishonest, at best and outright criminal, at worst.

Another related example of intellectual dishonesty is when people are "taught" to routinely say "I love you" to people when everybody knows that half of the time, it is not true. Children learn to tell their parents that they love them when half of them cannot "stand their parents". More than half of these children would not keep their parents in their house for more than a week. Yet they tell them every day that they love them. A good number of these children move out of State, when they grow up, to be as far away as possible from their parents, and in some cases their siblings. Some only call their "loving" parents only on their birthdays, thanksgiving, Christmas and perhaps one other holiday in a year if they are generous. And some don't call at all. If one of the parents calls on the phone, the son or daughter would want the conversation to be cut short because she/he can't stand her/his parent. Yet at the end of the conversation she/he will say: "I love you Mom/Dad; I miss you" and sometimes she/he would add: "very much" to the 'I love you, Mom/Dad'. First of all, if one cannot love ones parents, who else can one love? If one cannot stand ones parents, whom else can one stand? Psychologists call the "I love you" trend an affirmation. Yes, an affirmation is fine if it is real. The problem is that in America it has become a cliché in many cases. Many people get stuck with hearing only what they want to hear. From parents this falsehood is carried on to other relationships like friends and marriage. Another downside of this trend is that no one knows when it is true and when it is not anymore. It is as if everyone is expecting it. It has in many cases set the wrong foundation for marriages, which ended up in divorce and has caused the untimely deaths of many women in fake "I love you" relationships in this country. Many young women and teenage girls and boys have been killed by men, who have mastered the art of telling women and young boys what they want to hear and what they have been programmed to believe. Unfortunately they have believed and taken every "I love you" as true and real. Even when they know that it is not true, they just relish in the idea that the man tells them: "I love you"; and that he thinks that they are the most beautiful women or boys in the world. They have gotten used to it that they believe it when they know it is not true. Naivety, stupidity or both! A typical example is the popular song: "Tell me that you love me" even if you don't mean it. If "I love you" from a man just satisfies a girl's longing and ego, she will follow the man to any place under the Sun. Many times such girls are killed or raped. Some young teenage girls are lured into the 'mouth of the lion' because a man with a camera tells them that they look gorgeous like movie stars and asks them to pose for a photo on the beach or elsewhere. One line like this is all it takes: "Has anyone told you that you look like Actress...or Actor...?" The next thing is a promise to show them the ropes into Hollywood. With the bloated ego, these unsuspecting but stupidly naïve girls would go anywhere with a man with a camera. They would end up, and some have in fact ended up as sex slaves of such men in this country or overseas. "We are going to do some 'shooting' in Hong Kong," is all one needs to get an anxious and ego-driven teenage girl on the plane to the Far East into prostitution. While they are as far away as Hong Kong, the Police and all Law Enforcement people will be looking for them in the United States for months with tax-payers' money. Some sexual predators use the same tricks to get young boys, who have lost their personality, identity and self- esteem. This is the result of parents and society exposing children and young people to falsehood as a way to boost their ego; it is what happens, when one chooses political correctness in place of reality which is not flashy; it is what happens, when one has a false sense of the self with an insatiable appetite for external beauty as young American girls are made to believe these days. These Egocentrics think the best profession is to be a model and ultimately Actors and Actresses. They want to be watched as the center piece; they want to be the action to be admired. These are some examples of the problem created from the class room, where they are told falsehood about their grades or overall school performance to make them "*feel good*", to their homes, where nobody dares give them some corrections lest they be upset and call the cop on their parents on any accusations they made up. They already know that the government has given children an 80-20 percentage point advantage over their parent or parents, if they bring any accusation against their parents. This is yet another tool to further the damage which is done to naturally good and innocent children placed under the care of adult society.

Many of our marriages are built on this same falsehood and a total misunderstanding of what love is. If married people, who tell each other "I love you; you are the most beautiful man or woman that I have ever met", were real or if they meant what they said, why do we have fifty percent of all marriages in the United States of America end in divorce? Why do young people who say the same "I love you so much", "I can't live without you" to their dates go through fifty or seventy dates before they get married? Even then we don't know if the marriage will last. People, over the years, got used to saying things they do not mean because they don't want to upset someone. . How many cases of men, who tell their wives everyday that they love them turn around and kill them by themselves or through someone else? Where did the so-called love go? Like Tina Turner, we ask: "what has love got to do with it?" Actually, not much! That is the nature of many so-called marriages we experience today.

Practically all introductions by male guests of some game shows go like this: "I'm---; I'm married to my beautiful wife---with my two beautiful daughters, -- --and---" If that word "beautiful" was omitted, the man would sleep on the couch all that week. It is a cliché that must be used even if he does not see her as beautiful. That is an inferiority complex that has become endemic with disastrous consequences of producing mal-adjusted individuals, who will go for anything to feel good, feel recognized, or admired, real or unreal. The man could have introduced his wife and children without adding, "beautiful" to it. But he had to do that to make his wife feel good. The point is that it is not necessary for this audience to know how beautiful the wife and children are. Real life is not lived in "feelings", fortunately. People can no longer live with what they see to be true, but what they want to feel. You have to flatter them by telling them the falsehood they want to hear to make them feel good. The whole advertising Agency is built on this falsehood. The people are trained to make viewers feel bad about what they have now and feel good about what is being advertised. And boy, it works all the time. After watching a commercial, some people throw out their Television or bed or couch to go to the advertising store to get new and "better" or "new and improved" ones. A very good Realtor can buy off a house from such people at a low price, turn around and talk them into buying it back from him at a higher price and still make them feel good about it because he makes them *feel good*.

This deception is featured again on signs people post at the rear of their cars, vans and trucks. They give their insecurities away with signs like: "I'm the proud parent of an Honors Student at ------ Elementary or (High) School". After reading it one feels like asking: "Who is asking you? Who cares? Keep it to yourself." Sometimes these so-called "honors" students cannot write their names. But the sign makes Mom or Dad or Grandparents feel good. Some parents force some teachers to include their wards and children in the "Students Honors" list. It is good enough for them to buy the sticker and put it on all the cars in the house and get some for grand parents as well without any interest in the veracity of what the sticker represents. It is more the feeling and satisfaction of the parents' ego rather than the academic progress of the children that is important here. The proponents of this life style will defend their position by saying that it is good for the self-esteem of the children. That is a very typical example of putting the cart way, way before the horse. It is defeatist and history has shown that it has not produced the desired result and will not. It is like escaping into alcohol or drugs, to make some problem go away. It is about time to revisit and revise the curriculum in Universities that award psychology degrees in this country and elsewhere to take care of these anomalies and false teaching on self-esteem.

THE EVILS OF LUST IN OUR SOCIETY:

Lust is defined in the dictionary as a strong sexual desire without idealized or spiritual feelings; it is any passionate desire like lust for power. Right off the top, we see signs of ego manifesting itself in the definition of lust. Passionate desire for power is a component of selfishness, which opens the door for many other vices. The only remedy to lust is to practice restraint. Here again freedom comes in play. Restraint is a sign of and an expression of freedom, properly understood; it is independence and maturity. On the other hand the lack thereof of restraint, maturity and good judgment is the other kind of "freedom" rightly called licentiousness (freedom to do any and everything with out restraint or control). That is not freedom; it is slavery. Jesus said that only the Truth can set us free. And any one who sins becomes a slave of sin. Slavery is the opposite of freedom. Sin is to slavery what truth is to freedom.

As we observed before, it is the misinterpretation of freedom as in the First Amendment that is at the core of American problem of lust, physical and mental. The development of this philosophy on lust is the engine, which drives the sexual revolution of the American Society. It is because I am free that I can dress any way I like, speak any way I choose, drink, eat or smoke whatever I like, sleep with anybody I like, married or unmarried, heterosexually or homosexually. This is what many Americans call freedom; and what they are spreading overseas. This brand of freedom is nothing but slavery. As all those freedoms, so-called become a national philosophy, is there any wonder that the nation is full of complaints of marital infidelity, divorce, incest, rape, abduction of young women and children, over-populated prisons, to mention but a few effects? Lust for all these vices becomes normal, under the guise of First Amendment rights. That is how this Society is becoming extremely permissive. As the Nation becomes lustful, the national conscience of America becomes numbed. Bizarre sexual behaviors on the streets, gardens, and parks between boys and girls in elementary schools, young adult males and females, men and women, men and men, and women and women become regular and familiar scenes in University Campuses and different communities in America. As this life style becomes a national philosophy, the bizarre become normal. The same picture is seen on the television every day. People are desensitized by the murder, of little children by their parents and strangers alike, rape of seven year olds by fifty year olds reckless and senseless shooting of children in school by their fellow students etc. To present an ordinary commercial on television, the Advertisers have to make it sexual in order to appeal to the American people. What has an advertised car got to do with a very young, beautiful lady provocatively dressed? To a balanced person, there is no relationship. But for the Advertising Manager, and the audience they target, it means a lot. He targets the women to subconsciously think that they will look as beautiful as the beautiful lady if they buy the car and the men to think that they might go home with the beautiful lady if they buy the car. In each case the Advertisement wins because they know the psyche of the viewers. The nation breaks new obscene grounds every time. It is ego, false living and of course lust all rolled into one.

Just recently the Oregon Legislature passed a law allowing Entertainment Houses in the State to allow people to have Live Sexual Intercourse on stage as a form of entertainment for a fee. These Entertainment Houses could be located near residential homes; and that would not matter to the Lawmakers if children get access to these Entertainment Houses. The Attorney General or his

Assistant defended the law on Fox's "O' Reilly Factor" Television Show. Freedom of Speech and Expression plus the almighty Dollar! Why do the people of Oregon let this go down? To say anything against *this irresponsible behavior* on the part of the Legislators would be interpreted as violating other people's rights of free expression. When the national conscience of a nation becomes insensitive, all kinds of rights begin to pop up: Right to die, Right to rape, Right to polygamy, Right to kill, (no, we have that already.), Right to steal, Right to anything one wants to do. It has become an obsession, which is driving the wheels of the nation. Like every other thing in the system, no one who can change the prevailing philosophy, is ready to take the bull by the horn. There are some politicians, who don't like the way it is coming down; but they are very few. The question is: who would risk their career for such a cause? But what happens next if they do? They are voted out. It is too hot to touch and too risky for politicians to deal with. It would be a political suicide for any politician to propose a legislation to stop this insanity. There we go again, back to where we started.

CAN THE AMERICAN SOCIETY PREVENT RAPE?:

The legal dictionary definition of rape is an illicit sexual intercourse of a man with a woman without her consent or of a woman with a man without his consent. It could also mean doing violence on a *person* or country. Some people have lately added "without full consent" to the definition. In my view there is no need to make that addition because "consent" is consent. You will either give it or you don't.

It must be a devastating experience to be raped. It is a violation that only a psychopath and sick person can commit because it is an invasion of an individual. For our purpose here, rape will be used as illicit sexual intercourse without the consent of one party. Even though the society in various ways has helped to create these sick people, a rape is an act that should be condemned by all. One can easily put rape into two categories: Rape by a stranger and Rape by a familiar person or a friend. Most cases of rape are committed by men as opposed to women. So we will treat rape here as a "male problem" only since there are very few reported cases of women raping men for whatever reason. Using the first case, one might ask: what goes on in the mind of a male rapist? It could be a case of a rapist stumbling on a helpless woman unknown to him. It could also be a very well planned rape, where the rapist targets an individual woman or any woman in a predetermined place like a jogging trail or park or her home. This will be a calculated, premeditated act. When all the dots are connected, he strikes. In either case, the rapist is bound to have a very psychological problem, most of which, in my judgment, was fostered and nurtured by society standards of morality and worldly "freedom". There are many societies in the world that have the word "rape" only on the pages of the dictionary. People have taboos; there are simply things that are not done in some cultures. For some societies, rape is one of those taboos. But in America, taboos are nothing but "inhibitions to people's psychological freedom and growth". So from age one, children are let loose to do what ever their natural impulses demand. Parents let children jump on dinning tables, televisions and computers, fight with pillows and break windows to vent anger. The instinct not to take "no" for an answer is developed and nurtured in some individuals with a mixture of other problems. It must be in the rapist's mind that part of the American freedom means that one is free to take whatever one likes and admires *if one can*. Since there are no inhibitions or taboos to stop the rapist from doing what the rapist likes to do, it is logical in his mind that he should go ahead and have sex with this or that lady, especially to satisfy his ego and power to do so. His lust is re-enforced by the fact that his action does not elicit any atom of *shame* in him. So he does not care. He is conforming to nature and natural desires like any other male animal in the bush would behave when he sees a female animal of his species. In the rapist's mind he is entitled to a beautiful woman whether she agrees to have sex or not like in the case of a rooster, a ram or a lion in the forest. Reasoning is temporarily suspended. He begins to plan on how to get his victim. At an opportune time, he makes his move and a crime of rape is committed on an unsuspecting woman. Horrible! Horrible! Horrible! Yes it is horrible. In God's Reign, it is an abomination.

But let us face the facts. Collectively we have consciously and or unconsciously removed God from society and public life especially in our schools where children and young people should get their first lesson on respect for themselves, other people's things and persons. "Popular Psychology" has planted 'no fear' in children, no respect for age and authority; parents and of course, no shame. Teaching children that some kinds of behavior are shameful is regarded as a sign of servitude, popular culture would say. Above all we have implanted in our kids that America, being a land of the free gives us the power to be anything we want to be; dress any how we choose; do and say anything we want, anywhere we want. Now a young man grows up with these "aspects of the First Amendment" so called, and has "fun" with this jogging lady, whom he "liked" and we call it rape. Wait a minute! He does not understand and will not stop because he has been conditioned and programmed from a very early age to be that way – do whatever, however and with whomever. There is no amount of jail or prison time, which will un-program this individual unless he seriously and sincerely goes to Jesus for help. Perhaps there has been no father figure around him. There are no "nos" and no taboos or inhibitions in the dictionary that this society gave him from the beginning. Nobody told him anything when he was enjoying all these freedoms in the house growing up or later in life: smoking cigarettes and weed at thirteen, staying out late, drinking alcohol, dropped out of school, dating five girls or boys every weekend as the case may be, and dressing in the most bizarre outfit imaginable. These behaviors are all part of the American "freedom" that did not instill any "no" answers when he was growing up. Now society is about to lock him up in prison for rape for about seven or more years; and if there was any violence involved, it might double that number depending on the State where it took place. The offence is a very serious one; don't get me wrong. But looking at his history, who should take the greater part of the blame, America? We or the criminal?

RISKY AND DANGEROUS BEHAVIORS:

The other type of rape is when the victim knows her assailant. It is also commonly known as "date rape". This is a very tricky one to pinpoint or even discuss. Some of it is real while most of it is not, in my judgment. Let me begin by saying that extra marital affairs and premarital sex are wrong and sinful in my religion and perhaps, yours too. Therefore I do not contribute to the idea of sex between the so-called "consenting adults" as right or legal. Any sexual activity outside of marriage is sinful irrespective of what human lawmakers say. Having said that let me say that many sexual encounters described as rapes are insults on human intelligence. The two rape cases that come to mind immediately, for purposes of illustration, are the Desiree Washington v. Michael Tyson case and the Kolbe Bryant case. It beats my imagination that Michael Tyson went to jail in that case. The only wrong he did was having or attempting to have sex with a lady who was not his wife. For him it was a sin against God and his wife. Miss Washington was guilty of sin too. If that deserved prison time, two of them should have gone to prison for what ever time is stipulated. I was surprised that the jury did not ask themselves these questions: "What was Desiree going to do in the Heavyweight Champion's Hotel room at one or two o'clock in the morning, all alone? If Mr. Tyson was in the Hotel room with his wife, would Miss Washington have gone to visit Tyson there at that time of the morning? When she left her own Hotel room and entered the Limousine sent by Mike Tyson at that ungodly hour of the morning to visit Michael alone in his Hotel room, what was she thinking?" Did she think she was going for a Church Choir practice or perhaps paying a visit to her blood brother? Did the Jury really believe that this "innocent" Beauty Queen of her State was going to Mr. Tyson's Hotel room to discuss a boxing match? Where was her Agent? Did the jury think that they had some boxing deal that could not wait till daylight? It is naïve to think of any thing other than what happened. What did Mike's body-guards and limousine driver think that this girl came for? Why did she cry "foul"? Could it be business gone bad? There are many "rape" cases like that where the female does something stupid and presumes that the man will not do something equally stupid. That is dumb.

The same thing is applicable to Kolbe's case. What was the lady doing in Kolbe's Hotel room? If she works there, she was not on duty then; she did not know him before. What was a stranger doing with a Basketball Star, whom she knew was married? Was it sex and money or a foiled expectation? Her sexual history reveals that she wasn't the Novice Mistress of a Novitiate that some media outlets were making her to be. She wasn't singing in the Cathedral Church Choir either.

When the DNA results showed that she had sex already with two other men before the case in question, she withdrew her complaint and the case from Court. She was not a novice but a pro. But as an American woman, she has the "right" to cry "foul" because it was a politically correct position to be in. Going in, she, as a woman has at least 70% point lead over Bryant. This is the way powerful women organizations have designed it with lawmakers and the public. It is no longer a question of finding the truth; we already know the truth; the lady told us the truth. But let us go through the Court system anyway. This is the typical rape scenario. When the Defense moved in vigorously, the "un-named victim" saw that her free 70% advantage had slipped away she could not continue the case. Her identity was protected while Kolbe's name and photo were all over the place. He lost endorsements and almost his family. In the end she got some undeclared amount of money out of it just as Monica Lewinsky made a name and some fortune out of infamy. Who said that these things don't pay? Unfortunately and shamefully many Americans were on the side of the "poor girl", who was raped by a celebrity Basketball Star with a lot of money. But there were a few people who saw the dollar sign bold and clear. Again our position is that both the complainant and Kolbe should have been equally punished. Her identity should also have been made known. That is the only way men will keep their pants on and the ladies start to respect them selves. It will make politicians, who are looking for votes, act honorably. But that won't happen because it is not politically correct.

The public and the juries in these and similar cases think that, by taking sides with the ladies, they are preventing rapes from happening. On the contrary, it encourages the ladies to make daring, dangerous and risky attempts because they know that they have more than 70% chance of prevailing in a rape case true or imagined. Some times the ladies go home with the almighty dollar coming out of their ears; but some times they end up in body bags, if they are lucky to be found for proper burial. Losing even one lady is not a good thing. Risky behaviors don't pay all the time. This brand of ladies has been armed to do serious battle with men in good positions or in money. In the event of an 'adventure' gone bad, they know to cry "rape" and the game is on. A good attorney comes in handy. If the Jury had declared both Mr. Tyson and Ms Washington's behavior as foolish, stupid and without merit, the Jury shall have sent a message to some individuals in society that the American people are no longer going to tolerate nonsense. If Juries and public opinion punish such stupid acts, there will be lesser fake cases of rapes. Then there will be enough time and money to prosecute real cases of rape. Perhaps more lives would be saved. We know that these juries were doing and acting according to the laws and instructions that they have. Therefore the ball falls back to the Congress of the United States of America.

Because of the devastating effects of rape, some women have tried to take undue advantage of societies' outcry against rape. Some want to make quick cash and some are stupidly relying on the so-called "sex without full consent" excuse. As I said before, consent is consent. It is ridiculous for a lady to initiate and lead a man to a sexual act and half way through she says: "stop!!" and later claim: "I did not give full consent." It plays on the intelligence of society. It is silly that any group of people would make a law to encourage a woman to excite a man into sexual intercourse and half way through, say stop. If he didn't or couldn't stop, should that make the encounter to be called a rape? Is it difficult to understand that men and women are wired differently? Ladies should be made to understand that they should not get near the kitchen if they don't like heat. This is the only way society can help young girls, who may think that boys are like girls sexually. They are not. The safest way, however is: "don't play with fire, to begin with". If on the other hand you want to experiment with fire, what you see is what you get. Stop complaining. To continue with the current trend is nothing but arming women to do practically anything and get away with it probably because women in the past were exploited. Is that a pay back time for women?

There are some cases also where some people have been prosecuted for "raping prostitutes". How does one rape a prostitute, who is illegally soliciting for sex for money? Let me make it clear that nobody deserves to be raped or killed. I will also say something that nobody has mustered the courage to say. Nobody has a right to put herself in a dangerous situation and expect to go free of harm as a Constitutional right. It is fools hardy or even plain stupid for a lady to walk half naked on the street at night or one o'clock in the morning and expect that every man that sees her will treat her with respect or simply pick her up for "sex for money". Yes, some will and some won't. Just as she is stupid to put herself in that situation, there are some men stupid also to take her "for a ride". I can no longer waste more time and paper talking about "raping a prostitute". It is almost absurd to envisage that. ACLU and Feminist Groups will jump all over me for saying this. Before you say anything think about what I said. It is true that if any such lady thinks she has the *right* to walk half-naked on the street, in the same token there are some men who equally think that they have the *right* to grab any lady they can for sexual purposes. Who is right? Personally I don't care for either of them. But it is not a judicious use of tax-payers' money to prosecute such cases once the facts, of carelessness on the part of the lady, become clear. That is where society and government encourage evil and perpetuate crime and senseless deaths. Some people might think this is too harsh. But I say that not treating it so would only continue to pamper irresponsible behaviors and encourage prostitutes to roam the streets because they know that the City will pick up the tab. Such endorsements of prostitution remove sex out of marriage where it belongs and make it a casual and money making event and no longer something to look forward to with respect and dignity in the context of marriage.

Every society gets what it asks for. It appears that we, the American society, are willing to accept any kind of behavior until something ugly happens. It is okay for us if a group of Navy Officers assemble (Tail Hook) to drink hard, get drunk and exchange sexual favors consciously or unconsciously for three days. We pass it as okay because "they are adults" and we can't tell adults what to do according to "First Amendment rights". The Tail Hook episode is an annually authorized event by the U. S. Navy. Nobody saw anything wrong with it until some lady officers complained that they were raped. The media and the American society were fascinated with the news for about a year. It attracted Congressional Inquiry. Soon after the Tail Hook incident, other alleged cases of rape and sexual harassments by senior officers surfaced in the Army and other branches of the Armed forces. It has also been revealed that some Recruitment Sergeants in all the branches of the Military have asked sexual favors from female recruits over the years. Shocked? Not at all! The only accurate thing to say about it is that the involved Sergeants were simply being true to the society they live in. It was discovered that many of the superior officers, who got the complaints did nothing about them, probably because it was no "big deal" to them or they were living in 'glass houses'. Yes, it may not be anything too because generally in America, sex is no big deal. After all, "everybody is doing it", some would say. This of course, takes us to the question of "character" and good up-bringing in the home. To talk about character as part of what is essential for public office has vigorously been opposed by people, who say they are liberals. They want people to be "free". They insist that what is important are: "Can this officer or military person fight? Is he or she a good soldier? Can this President balance the budget? Is this politician able to deliver? Is he a good Scout Master, gay or not with young boys? You don't need character to do these." This is the liberal mindset. One can have moral and ethical behavior problems and still be a good and successful President or popular Politician or good officer in the Military. They want everybody to do whatever they want anywhere they want. For them that is the interpretation of freedom. And that is the problem with our society today. We cannot give everybody, including our public officials, a pass on behavior and expect the Military personnel to behave differently. They are Americans too. Remember that we took members of the Armed Forces from the public. If character and ethical behavior don't matter for the public, why should they matter for the men and women of the Armed Forces? So when a Training Staff Sergeant or high ranking officer asks for sexual favors to promote or else punish someone for not complying with "orders" or even going ahead to rape the individual anyway, why should we raise our eye brows? We cannot stretch freedom to that extent and still have justice and peace at the same time. We cannot be liberal to some and punish others for being liberal at the expense of another. The only solution lies on Congress to revisit the power of trial lawyers and ACLU and to interpret the First Amendment the way the Founding Fathers had intended. Such a Constitutional surgery will bring back character and decency to the table and rebuild the moral fabric of our society. Good will once more be good, and evil will once more be evil.

Part of my confusion is that the Tail Hook is an event that has been happening for years before the alleged scandal. The media have always known the immoral behaviors that characterized the event over the years. The word "immoral" is mine. The liberal media would not use that word to describe what went on in the Tail Hook event in question. So what is the media concerned with? It makes news. This society is thrilled by such news not because of their outrage or concern for the morality or lack thereof, but the thrill and sensation. Another area of my confusion is why the lady officers filed the complaint. According to the news, these lady officers were drunk as were the male officers. The lady officers left their floor and went to the male officers' floor when the supposed rape and or assault occurred. Who is the victim here? From the news report, both the male officers and the lady officers were under the influence of alcohol. Whom should we convict? Why did the ladies even file a complaint? Because they are women; I get it. If they could not control themselves, how do the ladies think the equally drunk individual men could control themselves? That again is the problem with "dancing with the wolves". We should all come out and condemn people deliberately engaging in risky and dangerous behaviors. Some things do not mix up well. Excessive drinking, perhaps drugs, men and women, all in one mix, are not a very good combination. Once again, if you are stupid enough to engage in a stupid and risky behavior, there will be equally some stupid people on the other side of the spectrum willing to engage. Solution: Fine the accuser and the accused heavily and dismiss the case. Three gavels! All rise. Case over! The two sides will learn some lessons. Don't drink and drive; don't throw a grenade in the fire place. That will help us to recognize and deal with real and genuine cases of rape.

A University student and a mother of two children recently alleged that she was gang-raped by three members of Duke University La Crosse team. She performed as an Exotic dancer for these players in an off campus house. This does not smell good. What is the objective or the rationale of a lady scantly dressed in her under wear seductively dancing for a group of young men off campus? Having fun? Making money? We, as a society, sanction certain behaviors, whose objective is very clearly not decent as ways to make money: this young lady is there to purposely wet the sexual appetite of teenager boys and young adult men with testosterone running wild. The young men and teens are there to enjoy the bait and give her money for whatever is their satisfaction. The more sexually provocative she is the more money she gets. In the same token, the more excited the men get, as a result of her performance, the more money they are likely and willing to give her. Is anybody confused about what is happening here? I'm not. So why do we entertain this outcry about rape? This whole thing is ugly, period. One might say that there are rules about touching and not touching of the dancers in these situations. Right! You might as well make a rule to drop a piece of meat to a lion in the cage and tell him not to eat it until you count from one to hundred. Is any one in doubt about how freely alcohol flows in such Exotic dancing places? When you mix drugs, alcohol and sex in that kind of environment, who is talking about rules anymore? It is like pouring a can of gas in a room, strike a match and throw it into that room and cry: "Fire"! If you can find a stupid lady willing to risk her life, her dignity and respect just to get money, you will readily find a stupid man who is willing to make a fool of him-self, for sexual gratification. I'm not interested in if it is true or not that a rape took place in a case of this nature. Dismiss such a case and stop wasting the people's money on stupid cases. The society should help our young men and women to make good choices and stop patronizing stupidity.

The same thing goes for the folks, who think they have "rights" to do all sorts of things and expect everybody to bail them out when crunch time comes.

Tobacco, Alcohol, And Illegal Drug Use:

For the past twenty years or more, it has become crystal clear that cigarettes and cigarette products are addictive and dangerous to human health. That means that anyone, who is forty years old and under has heard enough about this danger in school, church, on Television or knows some relative, a friend or someone, who died of emphysema or lung cancer. What would be the reason for anyone forty years old and under to start or continue to smoke today except that it is a sign of his freedom and also that the American people are there to pay for his hospital bill even when he goes to the Emergency

Room twice a month? What business has a teen boy or girl to smoke except to show that he or she is a free American exercising his or her rights under the First Amendment? What benefit does a lady get from smoking except to show that she can do what men do as a right under the First Amendment? As long as she can smoke, drink and drive a big ol' FORD F-150 or bigger, she has arrived in the man's world and achieved equality with men. Thanks to the First Amendment! It has been made perfectly clear that smoking not only eats up ones finances, it also eats up ones lungs and causes cancer in men and women as well as unborn children. Second hand smoking has also been proven to be dangerous especially to children in the homes and in cars. Yet some women continue to light up in their houses and cars with children in them to satisfy their "freedom", their ego, power and lust.

As if they need to prove something many boys and girls in High School smoke cigarettes and some do other drugs as the next step up after cigarettes to "get high". Like the women, who smoke, these young people think that they need smoking to be recognized as full adults. I've asked some young people of High School age why, knowing all the bad effects that cigarette smoking has on people, they still try to smoke. Invariably they have told me that it helps to calm them down. What does it calm them down from? What is the stress of a teenager, who is not paying for his room and board, school fees, clothes, not even doing the cooking or holding a serious job? The only thing that might raise some semblance of stress would be running around with boy friends or girl friends instead of concentrating on their studies. What a stress in deed! Is that enough reason for a teenager to start smoking? By the time they are in college, they have become addicted to smoking. There are too many things going on in the lives of High School students other than studies. Is there any wonder that 33% of American High School students drop out of school. It is unbelievable that in a super power like America, one High School student, out of every three, drops out of school. Why, one might ask? Is it because of lack of teachers, books or school fees? Of course, not!! There is too much freedom to self-destruct, unfortunately.

The same thing applies to people doing all sorts of drugs. None of these drugs is food. It is not like gaining weight by eating too much hamburger. These drugs are known to be dangerous going in. If one chooses to make doing drugs a way of life in spite of all the campaign against drug use, should one not be left to deal with it instead of spending time and money on someone who is not ready to cooperate with people, who are trying to help him? But unfortunately the "politically correct" people will encourage and aid them in all sorts of ways. Anyone, who distributes fresh needles or condoms to Addicts to continue in their habits, is an enemy to the addicts and society at large. He is doing nothing but digging their graves and asking them to jump in. Some times the only way to teach some people is to let them sleep on their bed the way they make it. While it may or may not help the immediate individual, it will surely break the cycle and provide a high potentiality of stopping others, who might want to go the same route. As they say in prison: "If you are old enough to do the crime, you should be old enough to do the time". Or "if you do the crime, you do the time". If one hangs on to what one calls "freedom", one has got to deal with whatever consequence that kind of freedom brings with it. Most Americans are willing to help the genuinely poor and needy, but not those who willingly and knowingly self-destruct. And any government encouraging that kind of behavior is willfully establishing a second wave of slavery in America. That is the quickest way to destroy a whole generation; it is the surest way to enslave the minds of the next generation. The healthcare costs alone from drug use and cigarette related diseases can cripple a nation and the drug culture will eventually install the devil, who will make zombies of most of its citizens. Then things will get ugly.

High School Senior outings and College Spring breaks are of late hitting the headlines. Sadly nobody, Politicians or Church leaders, has spoken up on the subject to draw some attention to the growing evil of Spring Breaks in this Nation. A lot of people including the media describe them as a way of "young people having fun". The parents, school authorities, State and Federal Governments customarily keep silent until somebody is raped and or killed. Then the liberal media, parents, schools and governments speak up and dominate the news for months. They will do anything or give anything to raise the issue to make political points. Sometimes they solve a case or two. But that is not the point. What happens to those who died? What happens to those cases that are now cold? It is my opinion that the old adages: "Prevention is better than cure" and "a stitch in time saves nine", should be our guiding and relevant principle to follow in these situations. If parents, governments, feminist groups, the media houses and ACLU were to exert one third of the time, money and energy they expend on promoting false freedom and put it on educating young people about real life out there and emphasize the advantages of decent living, we would not be having so many cases of premature deaths of young ladies. Some times the attention that these organs give when sad stories of rapes and or deaths of young ladies break is but a belated way of showing remorse and guilt on their part. Some times parents are so self-centered on themselves and their own pleasures and love exploits that they don't have time to train or supervise the children. In many cases the parents, who are either single or divorced have no moral values to hand on to these children, who begin to act up as a form of a reaction or revolt. Some of the children end up in very high risk behaviors that may lead to their demise. "Keeping Hope Alive" on the part of parents and society trying to solve a problem is not adequate and cannot remove the guilt. No solution of a crime of homicide will be as satisfactory to the victim's family as having their beloved one home safe and sound. No amount of money spent on attorneys and forensics will compensate for a lost human being. A fraction of the money would be better used paying for the tuition of these young people than millions of dollars without them. We are reluctant to use it on them when they are alive; but we are very ready to use it when they are dead. It is counter productive and waste of money to encourage young women into risky behaviors by cleaning up their mess and get them ready for another mess. One might say, "after all Uncle Sam is still alive". It is no secret that we as a society, pushed by the vocal minority and the "politically correct" wing on the left, have been giving all the wrong signals to young teens with respect to sexuality and free expression. For the unfortunate ones, the one sexual indiscretion may become their, perhaps one and only sexual encounter ever, because dead people do not have sex. These young people think that the venturing into risky behaviors is "their First Amendment rights". After all, they are Americans; they are young and nothing will happen to them even on foreign soil. But unfortunately some young men and drug dealers in these Island cities and Resort places lay in wait for "the crazy American girls", who will never be the same after the 'End of the Academic Year' outings or 'Spring Breaks'. It is unfortunate that many precious lives have been lost as a result of reckless behaviors sponsored and approved by parents and various authorities. We encourage the "Girls-gone-wild" foreign beach occasions as something to be proud of and a way of having "fun" for our children.

If these outings are well organized, there would probably be nothing wrong in High School students, having these outings, as part of their graduation ceremonies. Exotic Islands, however, would not necessarily be the best locations. But these resorts could still be tolerated if the intentions are clean and provided there is adequate supervision. Sadly enough, everybody is expecting the things that "go down" in these places. That may even explain why there is no real supervision. There is an *unwritten permission* to experiment on sex, drinking and perhaps, to do drugs as a form of initiation into adulthood – turning 18. For the teens adequate supervision would ruin the whole idea of outing, and parents and School Authorities seem to endorse and agree with the supposition. The impression so far seems to be to let the young people go to a place out of the prying eyes of parents, big brothers and big sisters and go where they can "let their guards down" and have "fun". What then is the outcry when "funny things" happen when people are having "fun"? I suppose we do not expect the ground to be *dry* when it is *raining*. Blood is not a surprise to anyone when one is stabbed with a sharp pointed kitchen knife. It goes with the territory; "fun" can be expensive.

What exactly is having fun? Who defines "fun"? Not everyone will sanction letting young people go on Spring Breaks to have this fun, which different persons have different definitions for. The next question to ask is: Is there any person who should be deprived of this "fun"? Most likely the answer to this will be, "No". Then since there doesn't seem to be any guidelines or clear cut definition of what this "fun" is, practically anybody can use their own definition. And they do. Who is then to say that the young man, who forces his way on a girl to have sex, is not having "fun" and exercising his First Amendment Right? As ridiculous as this might look and sound, it is very logical under the frame work we have lately used under the provisions of the First Amendment Rights (wear what you want to wear or go naked if you feel like doing so, do whatever you want to do, say anything you want to say, drink if you so choose etc). In that package, there is nothing stopping one from rapping someone if that is what they want at the time as their 'fun'. If it is sinful and wrong to rape someone, as it actually is, then something must be wrong with the way the First Amendment rights have been interpreted since the sixties and lately. It is such framework that gives birth to the so much used expressions like "fun". There is no doubt that school authorities and parents know what goes on in those outings and they don't care or don't mind. Perhaps they don't want to appear to be politically incorrect. It is pretty much like what happens in College Spring Breaks in some of these Exotic Islands, where anything goes; everything is fair game and it is all perfectly legitimate and Constitutional. Parents and Government Officials see it all play out on National Television. For the eighteen year old High School graduates, and College Students, High School outings and Spring Breaks are official initiations into the Age of Woodstock and Free Sex, the Age of 'Wisdom' and the Hippie Age reinvented. If society is willing to give their High School and College students the permission to go sexually wild, society should, in my opinion, shut up and stop complaining when someone rapes or murders a young lady in any of these risky environments because some folk might just be having "fun" doing just that. This, not only, sounds crazy; it is crazy and adequately makes my point. *Alcohol and dangerous drugs plus societal permissiveness have created monsters and sadists, who take pleasure in inflicting pain on others, trivializing sex and having a heck of time doing it.* Talking about risky behaviors, who would like to confront or mix up with people like that in the name of exercising ones freedom? Not anyone related to me, not a friend and surely not anyone I love!! That is why I would not want any of the above mentioned relatives to confront "these monsters" in the name of "Freedom" by getting involved in these high risk behaviors. It is like choosing to confront the devil, who is a powerful spirit and bad angel, instead of steering clear of him altogether. Is it a smart thing to insist on our "freedom" to do these things and become prey to such individual monsters, whom we cannot control? Or would it not rather be better to advise our children, especially the girls, to be more careful about where they go; what they wear and how provocatively they dress; what they drink and whom to go out with? We have lost too many young people because they did not learn that there is some price to pay for every act of freedom we exercise; that there is a consequence for every action we perform. For too long a lot of people, especially the ladies, have extrapolated from "sex without consequence" that there is something like "risky behaviors without consequences". We cannot guarantee that.

Talking about these cases of rapes and murders of these teenage girls, one feminist asked a very interesting question: "Who said that a girl should be raped or killed because she is drunk or under the influence of drugs in a bar?" The answer is very clear. Nobody should rape or murder any lady no matter how drunk or high she may be. But that is not really the issue. The real question should be: what kind of person would rape a lady in a bar, parking lot or gathering? Invariably it will be someone who is not mentally stable through the use of alcohol or drugs or someone devilishly obsessed with sex. Where do we find such people? It is mostly in such environments that promote promiscuity, public drinking like bars, strip clubs and drug activity places. If a lady willingly mingles with people in such places and gets involved with such behaviors that take place there, the result will not be shocking to anyone who wants to be realistic. No gentleman would rape a lady anywhere. Certain activities feature in certain places. Very often sexual activity, either consensual or rape, goes with the territory of drinking and drugs. So if you don't like the heat, get out of the kitchen. If we as a society say it is okay to liberalize and demean sex, advocate drinking and drugs; if we permit our children to get involved in high risk behaviors, as part of our "individual rights", we should just keep quiet when the next student is raped or killed in these high risk and sexually charged places. There are no guarantees in such places. Dumb people attract other dumb people.

Some statistics and surveys show that these students say that during Spring Breaks they consume four to five times the amount of alcohol they would normally consume elsewhere and about three or four times as many sexual partners than usual. But it is sad to say that some don't come back complete, safe or alive. The survey adds that a good number of the girls go back to school pregnant and some with a variety of sexually transmitted diseases. At the end of each Spring Break, a few more thousands of American babies are added to the abortion list and statistics. It is a hard reality that we all, especially those who make and interpret the laws and those who encourage these loose behaviors, will have to answer to God for on behalf of the children placed under our care. That a teenage girl during one of these end of year breaks is drinking and bouncing from one bar to another at night until the bars close about one or two o'clock in the morning is not seen as abnormal in our society today is a sad commentary on our society. It equally tells the story of what the next generation of Americans will be. The cost in man-power and dollars is enormous when something bad happens to one such lady, student or worker. Ironically it is none of society's business where a lady goes to drink, what she drinks or how much she drinks. But if she get into trouble or is killed doing it, it immediately becomes the business of society; the government, law enforcement and the people are ready to spend what it takes to prosecute the case. In it somebody makes political gains on tax-payers backs. It is very strange that the tax payer, who has no say in someone's risky behaviors, is called upon to foot the bill. No one will take out time to condemn the idea of people exposing and putting their own lives to dangerous situations. It is even sadder, that we let law enforcement people risk their own lives in order to save reckless risk-takers, who are exercising their First Amendment Rights at the expense of others. Will someone tell us: what is the wisdom of a teenager getting drunk on his or her 18th or 19th or 20th or even 21st birthday? The funny thing about it is that everybody seems to expect it. With reference to teens getting drunk on their 18th birthday, someone once told me: "it is what you do; it is just like getting drunk on weekends. You work all week and on weekends, you drink." Isn't that whole idea crazy? That is the beginning of the *dulling* of the conscience and *blurring* of ethical values, which begin to hunt individuals later in life, if they wake up, and sometimes it causes despair and drives many over the edge into sex, alcohol and drugs. When they have to choose between their obligations to God and a human being, they are more likely to choose or please man and displease God. Is there any wonder why about 30, 000 people attempt or commit suicide every year in the United States of America? With our education and wealth, should anyone have a reason to commit suicide? The reason we have this high rate of suicide is because we have ignored all the rules of reason and decency. By inviting and brewing chaos in the name of freedom and rights, we created and nurtured stress and depression. This prepares the way for people, especially young people, to act out as is shown in substance abuse of all types and sex as an escape. When they really find out that escape is a mirage, suicide ("to just end the heart ache") comes handy. In many ways we have all been part of killing a lot of people; some share a lot more blame than others.

Nigerian youths are very much catching on in all these areas. The spread of the American culture in Nigeria is very fast indeed. The young people are very much into many of the happenings in America. It is a scary development of events. It is easy for the rat to follow the lizard into the water, but it is not as easy for the rat to dry up as the lizard when they come out of the water. While there are no reported cases of sustained abortions, rapes, alcohol and drugs use among students in Nigerian schools as in the United States of America, one cannot assume that there are no such activities going on. It is not yet an issue probably because both the people and Government frown at such behaviors and attitudes. If any court or government gives them the go-ahead order 'freedom', there will be worse cases there than in the United States now. These organs – Parents Teachers Associations, Board of Governors, and the society - help to put a lid on the small number that may exist. It is the intention of the writer to expose the problems caused by these behaviors in the American society as well as the difficulty America is having in trying to combat them. The results are far-reaching and have been very entrenched in society for over forty years. Nigeria is better off without these imported social and moral problems because she has enough of her own kind of problems. Bribery and all forms of corruption are enough debilitating ills in Nigeria to be added unto. As a young and developing Country Nigeria does not have what it takes to handle the kinds of issues and problems that America is grappling with. The infrastructure is different; the student base is enormous. What a city in America uses to prosecute one student rape case will be more than enough to run a city of like size in Nigeria for a year. If a student drops out of college as a result of one of the hazards of a Spring Break, he or she has so many other chances and avenues to recovery in the United States of America. Community Colleges and remedial outlets are all over in the United States with State and Community financial backing. There is practically no social or government agency or support in Nigeria as one would get in say, a Community College in America. It is a terribly bad idea for Nigeria to import some of these cultures from America without a careful scrutiny.

CHAPTER SEVEN:
THE CHURCH AND THE STATE

The Church and the State have a very unique relationship. Strangely enough, this unique relationship is a surprise to a lot of American people, who have been hankering after the so-called "Separation of Church and State", which is not even in the Constitution. The ignorance of not recognizing this unique relationship is responsible for the so many misunderstanding and friction in the Church and State relations in which human beings are at the center. In a way, the Church is on the one side and the State is on the other of the same issue. They are the two sides of the same coin. The State and the Church meet on a common ground because they serve the same subjects, people. The people of God make up the State and the State serves the people of God. It is because of this that there could really be no "Separation of Church and State" proper. The State exists for the people and the Church exists for the people; the one takes care of the material welfare of the people while the other takes care of the eternal destiny of the same people. In a God- directed-society, (the way it should be) there could not be any dichotomy between the Church and the State. By design one is supposed to be subjected to the other for the wellbeing of the people.

The only reason some people in the American Society keep on harping on the so-called separation of Church and State is because they neither know the functions of the Church nor that of the State. It might have been Ghandi, who said that anyone, who does not know that every political question is a religious question and every religious question a political question, does not know the nature of either religion or politics. The concept of "Separation of Church and State" can only barely exist even in the mind. It has no practical application in real life. Anti-religious individuals and politicians use it to confuse people, who do not sit down to analyze the workability of such a concept. Lately some American politicians have created a barrier between the Church and State using the "Separation of Church and State" philosophy. The nation has started to produce individuals who have no morals, no values and no God as well as people who don't know if they are male or female because of this misconception in Church and State relations. There is a growing identity crisis in the Country because there is a general acceptance that God and religion are not necessary for the people. This concept, if it sinks in, can make somebody do the unthinkable because there is no looking forward to eternal destiny. That may be the goal of the proponents of a society without God. All children are made to go to school because it is necessary for the people and society. But for religion, it is the business of the churches. The real reason for the separation is that if the idea of God is stifled, these operatives will do whatever they like without "God watching" too closely. Wrong again!! No one can achieve the goals of the State without the understanding and cooperation of the Church and Church people nor can anyone achieve the goals of the Church in conflict with the good order of the State. That is why the Founding Fathers had a better grasp of what that relationship entails. The Bible and the teachings of the Church are in agreement that legitimate national leaders should be obeyed and supported in all legitimate endeavors because all authority comes from God. Jesus, the founder of the Church asked his disciples to pay taxes to the State. He paid taxes Himself. The Ten Commandments are all about how man should behave in society to be a good neighbor and a law-abiding citizen of the State and an instrument of God's Glory. The Framers of the Constitution knew this all along. That was why they insisted in the First Amendment that: Congress shall not make laws to establish a *national religion*. This counter balances with Congress shall not make laws that will *curb the exercise of religion*. They were right on the money then and they are right on the money now. Therefore there could not be a valid separation of Church and State all of which serve the same people.

THE RULE OF LAW:

Law is a body of rules that bind a group together. The existence of a law presupposes a law giver. There are laws and lawgivers of varying degrees. There are laws and rules in the family, Local, State and Federal Governments, Schools, Clubs, different branches of the Armed Forces, Groups and Associations. But only one has the power to be the Supreme Lawgiver. Every other law and every other lawgiver derives their proper power and legitimacy from *THE ONE LAWGIVER, GOD HIMSELF*. God is the Supreme ruler from whom every ruler on earth gets his power and mandate. Therefore an earthly ruler is as effective as he adheres to the rules and regulations of the Eternal Ruler. Every ruler that has ever been, explicitly or implicitly, has had that opportunity of ruling by the light of the Supreme Ruler. Implicitly God had put into every human being the natural law to guide one in dealing with others. Sometimes it is described as the "golden rule – do unto others the way you would want them do to you". It looks scanty and insufficient. But it is as extensive and sufficient as the explicit Ten Commandments God gave mankind on Mount Sinai. The Ten   Commandments were summarized into Love of God and love of neighbor. To treat others as you would want to be treated is like loving your neighbor as yourself. And to recognize some power higher than you, are the love and honor and worship due to God. These are the first three Commandments – Love of God.

The essence of governance is to maintain this golden rule. To do anything other than that is governing outside of God's law and taking a big gamble on life. All through history, some rulers have over the years resorted to taking that gamble. Instead of ruling on God's law, they manufactured their own laws and made themselves "supreme lawgivers" at different times in human history. For those who believe in the Bible, there are many such cases in both the Old and New Testaments. In each case, the anger of God visited on those tyrants. Some times this kind of behavior leads to the death of those rulers as well as numerous subjects. For anyone who does not believe in the

Bible, we have witnessed in our own times and in history such tyrants like Adolph Hitler, Joseph Stalin, Bendito Mussolini, Fujimori, to mention a few. These tyrants made themselves "supreme rulers". Those were in the era of kingships, dictatorships and despots.

Today we have other kinds of "supreme" rulers and lawmakers and interpreters of the law. In our present day democracies, some individual lawmakers and justices have assumed the role of the Supreme Lawgiver and have relinquished God's Commandments to the sideline. Some examples that come to mind immediately are the permission seven Justices of the Supreme Court of the United States of America gave and some Lawmakers today continue to give to women in this country to abort their babies at will. Another permission given by some Lawmakers would be the recognition of the same sex union as marriage in some States of the Union. These two examples go against God's law, ipso facto, which means that by themselves they go contrary to the laws of God and nature itself. You must have heard people say that nobody should tell homosexuals how to live their lives. The feminists have also said such things as: "nobody has the right to tell a woman what to do with her own body." Many politicians have said the same or similar things in campaign trails in order to win people's votes. In other words, we should not display the Ten Commandments because it belongs to religion and Church, not the State. Moreover some people say that they do not believe in God and nobody should force their own religion on other people. Good try, Mr. Big-Stuff! How about this: You shall not steal what belongs to other people? What do you say about: You shall not kill anybody? What do you say about: You shall not rape somebody? Do not tell lies; why is perjury an offense? What do you say about some man sleeping with your husband or wife? The list goes on. These are all in the Ten Commandments. Should we discard these laws because they are all in the Ten Commandments? What say you, Mr. Big-stuff? Don't you think that it should offend atheists to luck somebody up because he broke into the bank, or killed his neighbor or raped a child? By the way what does the Police Officer do to an atheist, who contravenes any one of the Ten Commandments since he or she does not believe in God? So what do you do, Mr. Politician? Are you going to discriminate against someone who does not believe in God by forcing him to obey the laws: you shall not tell lies against someone? Perjury! You shall not kill. Are you going to convict an atheist of perjury or stealing or raping or killing your son, Mr. Separation of Church and State Politician?

Some members of the United States Congress and other Congresses and Parliaments in the world have been playing God for too long now. Almost everyone in Congress condemns the repressive, Communist and Totalitarian Governments in Russia and China, which forces abortion on women and limits the number of children a family could have. But is that system too far removed from what we practice here in the United States of America if the end result is the same – killing innocent babies? What is the difference between the Chinese Government forcing a woman to commit abortion and the American Government give permission, and in some cases, fund abortion on American women and women abroad? Is there any difference in forcing someone to kill a man and giving permission to someone to kill a man? They all enjoy the blessings of the State and are legal. No one can prosecute the Chinese midwife or doctor, who kills the second or third baby of a village woman who came to the hospital to deliver her baby just like no one can prosecute the abortion doctor in the United States for killing a couple of babies everyday in his clinic. In spite of all that we condemn China for limiting the number of children in each family.

America has in many ways, conditioned American families to a child or two per family; she has glorified single womanhood, single parent hood without a husband and entrenched abortion on demand mentality if pregnancy results. What is the difference between these and the Chinese situation, where the population is over a billion people? What is the American excuse? Practically the result is the same – children are being killed. This kind of behavior has one obvious conclusion: God's anger, sooner or later! As was mentioned above, many Empires have risen in history and are no more today because of the intransigence of the rulers of those Empires. From the look of things, America will not be any different unless there is a change of heart on these and other issues that go against God's Commandments. No man can legitimately make laws that contradict God's law, no matter how liberal and accommodating one wants to be of others. Therefore individual citizens are not bound in conscience to obey such laws. In the same way no individual, who has reached the age of discernment, can claim ignorance or defend his or her action on the grounds that it is legal in the State or the Nation to go against God's law. As a general rule, no law can be valid if that same law is contrary to the law of God, the only Lawgiver. That should serve as the rule of thumb. The whole idea of the rule of law is based on the premise that the law must be first of all just. It would not be just to pass a law that says: "If a father returns from work with out ice cream or candy for his son, he (the son) has the permission to kill his father". Or if a unanimous decision of the Supreme Court says: "If a lady is not ready to raise a child at this time or if a teenage girl is ashamed to be seen pregnant etc, the baby in the womb can be aborted." Or that by a unanimous vote in the Supreme Court, "men of a particular race in America should not be admitted into any University in the United States of America". Those are all unjust and non-binding on the citizens because neither the Supreme Court nor the Legislators have any power to make laws against the Supreme Law maker. Somehow, it is easier to pass a judgment when the example is far out there. What do you think about this law: "It is unlawful for any woman in China to have more than one child? If a woman has two children, one must be killed?" Are these just laws and why? So before anyone begins to enforce the rule of law, the law itself, must be just.

LAW ENFORCEMENT AND THE CRIMINAL JUSTICE SYSTEM:

The first job of the State is the protection and the welfare of the people of that State, born, unborn, male, female, young and old. This is a God-given duty of every State. Here the State is representing God as parents represent God in raising the children that God gave them. The President of a Country and the Congress or Parliament or the Governor of a State and the State Assembly and the Law-makers become to their people what parents become to their children. When laws are made, they must be enforced in order to realize the intended goal, which is to protect the life and property of God's people in that Country or State. That is why it is necessary for all citizens to respect and obey the laws of the Country and the State as coming from the Eternal Lawgiver. All authority of Government comes from God.

That is why all laws are supposed to be just laws because God is Just. Hence every individual is expected to pay their due taxes for the maintenance of the State.

The police have the duty of maintaining law and order in the State. In order to do this job well, the police should get all the help they can get from government. In fighting crime the government should give the police enough powers to do their job well. They must be well armed to combat the bad guys on the street. If they don't have adequate mandate to save their own lives and those of the people, maintaining peace will not be a reality. The Policeman or woman is somebody's son or daughter, somebody's father or mother, somebody's husband or wife. If the gang members have more Constitutional protection than the police, there will be no end to the gang culture and the effectiveness of police protection will be diminished. It is a shame that government does not even want to aggressively deal with the evils of gangs in the nation because everybody is afraid of ACLU. Gang members will put police on notice that they will demonstrate and get away with it under the First Amendment right. So what is the use to society of membership in a gang to earn them the First Amendment right? What else do they do except "decorate" the city with graffiti, hate another group or race, kill, do and sell drugs, set the homes and churches on fire and bring down the price of homes and business in the neighborhood and make teens drop out of school to join them? What is so honorable about this to make a group have such sacrosanct rights? That is why I still insist that we need to revisit some or all of the Amendments especially the First. It is very frustrating that the police will see people killed by gangs in a drive-by shooting and know almost all the gang members in a particular area, but they will not be allowed by law to make arrests because that would violate the gangs' rights. Meanwhile the innocent by-standers, men, women and children are dead without any First Amendment rights of protection. It is a shame. Sometimes the cops are killed by gang members who are not supposed to carry guns but they do anyway. How can any Cop enforce the laws under these circumstances: the criminals have rights but the victims have none, the gangsters have rights but the Cops have none? It is a very dangerous and disturbing trend where crime pays. These are realities that are defended in

Courts under the name of the First Amendments Rights. This may be one big reason why recidivism rate is high in our State and Federal prison systems. They have friends in the politicians and the ACLU. But victims of their onslaught have none. Who says crime doesn't pay? Only in America!! Only in America!!

How can the law enforcement do their job of protecting people when there are interpretations of laws that empower criminals to continue to menace and harass society? Some times honest people are tempted to engage in criminal acts because it appears that "crime pays". A man was hauled into jail because he shot an armed man, who came to rob him in his house. The house owner had a registered gun but the thief had a stolen and illegal gun. Why would a man defending his house, wife and children go to jail for it, even for one night? The thief was taken to the hospital in an Ambulance. His treatment and all were paid for by the State. But the house owner slept in jail that night. Who said that crime does not pay? Only in America!!

One Dr. Terry Bennett from New Hampshire was taken to court by one of his patients because he honestly told his patient that she had to lose weight if she wanted to live. She was obese and was not following the doctor Bennett's orders to lose weight. She felt insulted and sued her doctor. What is it that this patient wants? This is the case of the dollar sign all over the place and we condone it. What was the doctor supposed to do? It is unbelievable that a lawyer accepted to sue someone on behalf of this kind of client? It is all money; and crime pays. Lord, have mercy!!! Where are we going as a nation with the First Amendment and where did reasoning go? Anyone can almost sue for anything under the First amendment and win. This is justice in a justice system?

There have been several cases of individuals, who sued restaurants or Fast food places for some frivolous reasons. In one case someone sued a restaurant because a cup of coffee spilled on his or her lap or hands or that the coffee burned his or her lips. In each case, the plaintiff asked for millions of dollars in compensatory damages and many won ridiculous amounts of money. These awards are given by courts in most cases. Where is the justice? Are people supposed to buy coffee to pour it on their laps? Even in the shower people are supposed to check how hot the water is before they start taking shower. So far nobody has sued the shower yet for producing water too hot. I guess any litigant will collect millions of dollar if he sues. Only in America!!

There was a case of a couple, who acquired a finger from a friend, who accidentally severed one of his fingers. They took it to a Hamburger place. When they were served, they put the severed finger in the hamburger and drew the attention of the manager of the place. For a while everybody thought they were sitting on a pot of gold. Later on the truth came out. If the Burger place had not insisted on getting to the bottom of it, that fraudulent couple would have made away with a bundle of the almighty dollar. The Court would have awarded the couple some millions of dollars. The two people are now doing time in prison.

Let us not forget an individual who sued a Hamburger place because he was overweight. He ate hamburger everyday for many years. He accused the owner of knowing that the ingredients in hamburgers make people fat. What a discovery! He should have received a Nobel Prize for that brilliant discovery. Have we become a Litigation Nation because of the First Amendment or because of Trial Lawyers?

It is amazing that America, which is the most sophisticated Nation in the world, has the most criminals in the world. Instead of getting better, it is getting worse. The April 28, 1991 FBI report states increases in crimes in the United States in 1990 as follows:

Violent crimes up by 10% to 1,810,000 incidents
Murder up by 10% to 23,600
Rape up by 9% to 103, 000
Robbery up by 11% to 642, 000
Aggravated assault up by 10% to 1,050,000
Burglary down 4% to 3,040,000
Theft is unchanged at 7,872,000
Juvenile crime up by 23%

As usual, America is leading in the number of Inmates in the world. The 1992-93 figures are as follows:

United States has 1,330,605 Inmates.
Russia has 829,000 Inmates.
India has 196, 221 Inmates.
Brazil has 124, 000 Inmates.
South Africa has 114, 047 Inmates.

According to the 2006 revised numbers, the number of Inmates in the United States of America is estimated at 2.2 millions.

What is responsible for America's crime rate and increases? Like every other problem in this country, everything is related to everything else. If there are some people who have the courage to fix one area of the problem there will be a chain of reaction in the right direction. The election of seriously minded Legislators in Washington DC and all the State Capitals of the Country will be one way to go. We need to elect men and women, who have the interest of the people at heart; men and women, who are not watching the polls before they sneeze; men and women, who are not afraid of telling the people the truth even when it hurts; we want men and women, who like St Thomas Moore, was willing to say 'no' to King Henry V111 and 'yes' to God; we need men and women, who are willing to loose an election because they told the truth to their people about what should be done to fix this Nation. We do not need too many electorates in each Constituency, who would prefer to be told lies in order to make them feel good. Finally we need men and women, who are not afraid to revisit and re-evaluate the Constitutional Amendments with particular reference to the First Amendment. The abuse of the First Amendment is the root of America's social and moral problems, which impact on all other aspects of American life including the prison system. It is then and only then can this Country begin to recover some of her glorious past and drastically cut down on the social ills and crimes that have bombarded every city in this country.

It is my belief that no child is born a criminal. That is to say that every child is innocent until they come in contact with adults. Children have no discriminatory minds until an adult implants the idea in their mind. They will play with each other until their Mom or Dad tells them not to play with this or that child. Naturally children are color blind when it comes to people and race; they don't worry about their sexes until some adult brings it into focus. How do many of American kids end up on the wrong side of the law? Once again the answer lies in the adults in their lives: the parents and grandparents, teachers in their lives, Local and State Governments, all the levels of the judiciary, and finally, the Congress of the United States of America. Collectively all these different arms, consciously and unconsciously, mould innocent children to become criminals. It is unfortunate but true. We have discussed above how the absence of God in a child's life can create a perpetual vacuum that can never be filled by any other thing but God. It was St. Augustine who said that our hearts are restless until they rest in God. It is of such restless hearts that serial and callous, insensitive killers and rapist-killers are made. That is why we cannot divorce God from the State, the people or the school. Life has no meaning to killers and they don't care about anyone for that matter. Consequently there is nothing to dying or killing because they have no one to answer to. The one concept of no God is enough to create all kinds of monsters and criminals. It is also the foundation of bad laws that create these criminals to begin with.

MIRANDA V. ARIZONA AND THE FIFTH AMENDMENT:

There is some confusion in the interpretation of the self incrimination law and the delivery of justice. How does the Fifth Amendment insure that justice is done? The question before the Justices of the Supreme Court in 1966 was: are statements obtained from a defendant in custody without his attorney present and without a waiver on his part, of that right admissible in court? The Court had dealt with a similar question in Illinois in 1964, where the Court said that it is illegal to admit into evidence a confession obtained by police during interrogation of a suspect, who was denied a request to talk to his attorney. Before they gave their verdict, the Justices looked at three other similar cases. The first one was Vinera v. New York: Here the defendant made some admissions orally to the police during interrogations. Later that evening, after an interrogation by the Assistant District Attorney, he signed an incriminating statement. The next case was Westover v. United States, where the defendant was handed over to FBI Agent by the local police after they had detained and questioned him for a long period of time at night and the following morning. After about two more hours of interrogation, the Agent got a signed statement of guilt from Westover. The last question they looked at was California v. Stewart. Here the local police held the defendant for five days in police custody and questioned him on nine different occasions before they got an incriminating statement.

In the majority opinion the Justices believed that, because these defendants were either poor or uneducated, they were probably coerced into making or signing incriminating statements or confessions. Writing the majority opinion Chief Justice Earl Warren held that prosecution may not use as evidence in court statements obtained as described above unless prosecution can show that all safe guards vis a vis the self incrimination of the Fifth Amendment is guaranteed. These are the guarantees: Prior to any questioning initiated by law enforcement officers, after a person had been taken into custody, the person must be warned that: 1. He has the right to remain silent; 2. anything he does or says may be used as evidence against him; 3. he has a right to the presence of an attorney during questioning; 4. if indigent he has a right to a lawyer without charge. Unless the defendant receives these four warnings, the court would assume that any statement he made was coerced and therefore inadmissible as evidence in court. From an observer's point of view, the very wording of "Miranda" is very friendly to the suspect. Understandably there is a concern here for fair treatment of a suspect, who is innocent until proven guilty. But the pendulum of a rightful consideration has swung too far on the side of the suspect in the exclusion of the victim. That is the only problem in Miranda. Some times things happen too fast; some times the momentum of finding the truth is lost by delay. A kidnapped child or woman may be killed because of Miranda protocol. We are not here advocating that suspects be forced to admit a crime they did not commit. Not at all! That would not be justice either. Giving an Attorney to an indigent suspect is a good thing too. But to discard a true confession because his Attorney was not present goes over the top on the other side. One wonders: what is the object of the Criminal Justice System in this Country? Is it an objective and intensive search for the truth or is it a game of who can best outmaneuver the other? If it is the latter, "God save the queen". Then I would humbly suggest that "justice" be removed from the Criminal Justice System.

There has been some outcry about the Criminal Justice and the rich people, who get into trouble. The insinuation flies in the face of "justice" in this country and that is not a good commentary. If technicalities are more important than the truth, then it can be officially said and endorsed that rich people, who become suspects when a crime is committed should not even be tried. Being rich would become a technicality category, which would acquit. Did the five Justices consider that there are some criminals, who know the system and laws so well that the police cannot get any truth from them during interrogation within the Miranda context? This brand of criminals knows how to hold out, make deals and maximize the Miranda loopholes. That would not exactly be called justice.

In three separate dissenting opinions, Justices Clark, Harlan, Stewart and White disagreed with the majority on various constitutional and public policy grounds. In his dissent Justice Clark said that the majority erred "in one full sweep changing the traditional rules of custodial interrogation which this Court has for so long recognized as a justifiable and proper tool in balancing individual rights against the rights of society."

The majority opinion was afraid that suspects may be convicted falsely and there are some merits to that. By the Miranda rule, was the majority opinion also afraid that a criminal rapist or murderer may be set free? In trying to fix that, the majority has also made some mistakes of creating an avenue where real criminals may go free on technicalities. That is no solution to the problem of creating a level ground for equal justice. In the three cases before Miranda, there was no evidence that there was any sign of impropriety on the part of either the police officers or the FBI Agent. Trying to get the truth out of a suspect by questioning him in the morning and evening or for five days does not seem to be an offence. There didn't seem to be too much problem to fix in the first place. As Justice Clark pointed out, the Court had been served by these laws and techniques for many years. As it is now a criminal, who confesses to a heinous crime, which he or she really committed, may go free simply because he was not read his rights under Miranda. That would constitute a travesty of justice. Someone could commit murder with intent and go free on a Miranda technicality. At best Miranda is a decision of five over zealous Justices of the U.S. Supreme Court. In trying to punish the police, these five Justices have succeeded in punishing the society at large. In trying to give suspects a fair shake, they have erred on the side of the suspect. I wonder how one or all of the Justices would feel if one of their relatives or daughters were murdered and the killer gets off on Miranda technicality.

The Fifth Amendment states that a suspect may not make a statement or answer a question, which might incriminate him in a Court of justice. I don't know why the Fifth Amendment was put in the Constitution. It seems to encourage "not telling the truth". So, why does the Judge ask someone if he is guilty or not, if he was not supposed to incriminate himself even if he is guilty? It does not look as if the Founding Fathers wanted the "truth and nothing but the truth" in squeezing the Fifth Amendment in the Constitution. In a sense it resembles the way some people use the "Attorney" these days. The whole idea of someone, who knows the law to be an advocate to a defendant, was to be sure that he or she understands the laws as they apply to him or her and to make sure that the prosecution team does not pull some wool over his or her eyes. It is by no means a way to make the truth a lie or a lie, a truth. It is to make sure that justice is done on both sides. That is the wisdom of providing an Attorney to a defendant if he or she cannot afford one. The essence of the "Criminal Justice System" is to administer "justice for all" by setting the innocent free and punish the guilty. But there is an impression in the American Criminal Justice System that seems to suggest that if one commits a crime and has money to hire a top of the line team of Attorneys, one won't be convicted. That and the Fifth Amendment seem to defeat the whole purpose of a Criminal Justice System. To ask one not to "tell" the truth for fear of self-incrimination and to set one free because one has money is outright wrong. To convict one, on the other hand, because he doesn't have money for a better representation, is simply unjust too.

VIOLENCE:

Violence is described as the use of physical force so as to damage or inflict injury; it is an abusive use of force; it is a way to violate, to desecrate. To destroy out of malice and with force is violence. The use of force is something practically everybody hates. Most people the world over would admit that violence is wrong.

Implicit in violence is an element of terror brought about by the suddenness and unpredictability of the attack or violence. The fear factor of a terrorist act is at the core of the heinousness of terror or violence. That is why people are more terrified by the unknown, uncertain or threat of violence than the already experienced violence. The torture of expectation or lack thereof is more devastating than the terrorist act itself. All these aspects of violence or terror make them very unpopular in most civilized societies. When a violent husband returns home, fear grips his wife and children. That fear in itself is more damaging to the household than the violent acts perpetrated against them. The situation reminds one of what Shakespeare describes as cowards dying many times before they finally die. That is how powerful the fear factor or the surprise element is in people in violent situations. They 'die' many times before the husband/father does anything to them. This is also the inherent nature of gorilla-warfare and terrorism, the likes of 9-11 in the United States, terror acts in Spain, London, Indonesia, Russia and so many more all over the globe. In other words, violence is undesirable and disgusting.

VIOLENCE AGAINST WOMEN:

There are all kinds of violence. But some are more odious than others. If a man does a violent act against another man, it does not elicit as much odium as if a man does violence to a woman. Why is that? All over the world, women are regarded as more delicate than men. On account of that, women have some respects and privileges that are not generally extended to men, and rightly so. In some respects men are expected to take care of themselves. Violence to the weaker sex is not only unjust but also a cowardly act. Nature designed it that a man should safe-guard and protect his wife even with his own life, if need be. That was why in many, many years gone-bye, men carried the sword to protect their wives on the streets against wife snatchers like pirates and bandits. That was the origin of why the woman always stayed on the man's left so that he could use his left hand to push his wife behind him and use his right hand to hold his sword to ward off an assailant, wife-snatcher or bandit. It was an act of chivalry and courtesy to respect women, do simple courteous acts of letting women go into the house first, get seated before the men etc. In those good old days men would open the door to the house or to the car for the ladies to enter. It was a gentlemanly thing for men to treat the ladies with gentleness and respect. Violence to the ladies was not, and I suppose, is still not compatible with being a gentleman. There has been an unfortunate development in recent American history. The shift in attitude seems to be linked with the social and sexual revolution of the sixties, when women declared their independence. When women did everything in their power to look and act like men, courtesy to the ladies went down the tubes. The "new woman" started to regard what used to be courteous at a time, to be an insult in the new environment. Women started to drink and smoke heavily like the men. These substances react more strongly in women than in men. Women in the Military wanted to go for combat, cohabit with men in small and crowded ship compartments and the whole nine yards. And they got it. As a result, America produced her first set of new women, who do unusual and unwomanly things, which started a number of anti-societal behaviors. As we enunciated before: where there is a stupid woman, there is a stupid man close bye. Some stupid man broke the rules by being violent to a lady because the lady acted in a manner inconsistent with the normal and womanly behavior; violence to women took a prominent turn in this society, alcohol and drugs notwithstanding. No matter what the excuse is, it is still regarded as evil and uncivil, in civilized societies of the world for a man to lay his hands on a lady. But who can guarantee that it does not happen in a land where everyone thinks he/she has a right to do or behave anyway possible.

Violence against children is even on a higher scale in terms of disgust among people. Women can at least put up a fight in their own defense. Children are even more defenseless; and therefore they need a lot more protection than women. That all children are precious, is a given in many societies. Anyone who injures a child always receives the anger not only of the parents but of every one. This explains why everybody is on fire whenever there is a case of molestation or violation of a child in our society. Is there any wonder why, even in Prisons across the United States, "child molesters" are targets of other Prison Inmates? Prisoners, including those, who are murderers themselves, would mercilessly kill another Inmate in Prison for molesting a child. I guess there is something about a child that is sacred, innocent and inviolate. One crosses a clearly delineating boundary when one harms an innocent child. It is one of the offences that the Bible describes as crying up to God above for vengeance.

Violence against the unborn is at the apex of man's inhumanity to man. In the commission of violence to a man, who can put up a fight, we as society condemn it and with one voice say that violence is bad. In the commission of violence to the weaker sex, who can also, but to a lesser degree, put up a fight for her life, humanity says it is unacceptable. In the commission of violence against a child, who to even a lesser degree still can defend himself or at least can run away, this society rightly declares it horrible and unacceptable. If this violence is perpetrated by parents or relatives, the child is taken away from the parents or relatives and handed over to the custody of the State and eventually to total strangers through adoption. But in the commission of an unprecedented violence against the unborn, who are completely and unequivocally defenseless, *the out cry is not overwhelming.* This is puzzling as well as disturbing, to say the least. Nothing can be as inconsistent as the public response and reaction are not overwhelmingly unanimous. *Non violence is good for every other person except the unborn, who could not even be accorded the right to be born. Everyone has all kinds of rights under the First Amendment; but the unborn has not even the right to see the light of day.* Their lives are cut short violently, not by strangers, not by aliens unknown to them, (and there would be a prosecution in court); no! It is their flesh and blood; their own mothers and sometimes their Dads, who have refused to acknowledge their humanity in order to have the heart to carry out violence on them with "clear consciences". Could one have a clear conscience after killing a child? That is not possible. Can one propose and defend "a woman's right' and deny a baby's right to live and still have a clear conscience? No, somewhere, somehow, the woman must remember and weep secretly for her flesh and blood no matter how she pretends to have a clear conscience for killing this so-called "non person" inside of her. No matter how long it takes, it will happen. How long can a nation pretend to think that denying a baby the right to be born is a legal right and some kind of exercise of freedom? It will not be for ever. One million three hundred thousand babies are denied the right to be born in the United States of America every year since Roe v. Wade on January 22, 1973. That is a population greater than many nations of the world. This violence cannot continue indefinitely if we call ourselves a nation *of law and order*. If we can argue that terrorists and enemy combatants have a right to legal representation, why can we not dismantle a law that refused to accord some of us the unalienable right to be born? We have condemned people like Scott Peterson to die for double homicide – for wife, Laci and unborn child, Connors. We recognize Scott's son in the womb as a human being and turn around and say that the other child in the womb is not a person. When are we going to make up our minds? Or did we know all along that the baby in the womb is a person but can't say so because it might cost us some responsibility, some pleasure of political seat? We are all hypocrites, who give rights to all kinds of animals in the wild but cannot let our own flesh and blood be recognized as having rights as persons.

MAN V. ANIMAL:

In the Creation story in the Bible, God created a variety of different levels of creatures: the heavens and the earth, the light and darkness, day and night, all kinds of fish and birds, all other animals in the forest and finally man.

For most people in the world, man is the highest creature on earth not because he is the biggest in size; but because he is the only one that can reason and exercise his intellect and will. For those who believe in the Bible, man was the last thing that God created. In His image he created man and gave him authority over all other creatures. He gave man permission to rule and conquer the earth. Unlike animals man is accountable for his actions because he has the freedom to choose right from wrong. On account of his freedom, man can have assets and liabilities, rewards and punishments. When man was given dominion over the whole world, he was asked to use the things in the world for his upkeep. It is evident from man's position that he has a higher calling than, say, the animal. The preservation of the animal kingdom is for the good of mankind. That is why man takes care of the environment to take care of the animals to take care of man in order for man to love and worship God. It can be accurately said that animals were meant for man and not man for animals. But there is enough room for the co-existence of both animals and men just as God has ordained it.

But in recent years, there has been, in the increase, a growing number of animal rights activists, who have skewed the priorities in nature giving animals the place of man in the world. When there is a choice between animals and man, the choice should be clearly in favor of man. There should never be any hesitation in making the choice. Animal activists have gone so far as to accord animals more rights than man. That is as insane as it is absurd. This madness has gone one step below the theory of humanism, as a practical or functional system. The people, who are fighting to keep animals alive, are the same people, who are killing or advocating for the killing of one million and three hundred thousand innocent babies in the womb every year in America. What's up with that? If there is some consistency in their approach, one would have some sympathy for the activists and their love for animals. It is morally incomprehensible for Congress to make laws in order to protect endangered species of animals, but is happy that 1.3 million babies a year in the United States of America have had no protection since January 22, 1973. There is, however, nothing wrong in protecting endangered species of animals. But protecting animals in the bush with congressional laws and do nothing about innocent and helpless babies in the womb, is unconscionable. It is nothing short of the Pharisees and Leaders of the Israelite people asking for the release of Barabbas, the criminal and asking for the crucifixion of Jesus, who is not guilty of any crime. "Don't kill our animals and trees; instead kill our babies in the womb." This brings to mind the example of some millionaires, who set aside millions of dollars in their Wills for animals and pets while there are millions of children dying of hunger all over the world.

There is something very wrong with that misplacement of priorities. No matter how one loves his pets, no matter how important one thinks it is to protect these animals, they are still not human beings and should not be treated as such. Millions of dollars and thousands of hours were spent a few weeks ago to rescue a green whale off the shore near the Houses of Parliament in Britain; people cried bitterly when the whale died; yet no one seemed to care that 4,000 babies died that day and everyday in this country through abortion. There should be an attempt to balance our concern for every creature on earth, each to what it deserves. The preservation of the environment is as important as God has ascribed to the environment and man as God has allotted to him.

SECULARIZATION:

The same balance that is expected in nature is also expected to be between the Church and State. None should exist without the other since both serve the same man. The soul (anima) of man is encased and protected by his body. In the final analysis, it is man's Soul which will, rendezvous with God. Therefore it can accurately be said that the flesh is there to protect the soul for this end. It is very ridiculous to conjecture that it is unconstitutional for the State to help the Church to perform this duty. Instead America in the last thirty to forty years, has favored secularization against spiritualization and Faith on which the Country was founded. One big player in this is the American Civil Liberties Union (ACLU). This organization, which is made up of people, who profess atheism and people, who have little or no Faith or any strong sense of the Divine, has succeeded in moving America to the extreme left. This organization has helped many people to move away from the divine and the spiritual. For them everything has to be explained by matter. Consequently Faith, Religion and Church would not have a place in America, if they can get their way. Even then they are chipping away slowly but steadily at any traces of Faith, Religion and Church in the Country. Regrettably they are using the very words of the Founding Fathers, who were religious and spiritual people, to erode the very things the Founders wanted to accomplish in the Amendments to the Constitution. Sheepishly as if blindfolded, many American people are following this organization, some willingly and others, reluctantly.

The ACLU, Planned Parenthood of America and the National Organization for Women have been relentlessly fighting to secularize America. The ACLU, PPA and NOW derive their power from the job they do. They appeal to the baser instincts of man – the sexual appetites of man. Their aim is to bring society as far away from God as possible in order to be free from the promptings of conscience. For them this state is the ultimate freedom. It also explains why they use "freedom" as contained in the Amendments to make it happen. In the long run, man is man and animal is still animal.

SECULARIZATION AND RELIGIOUS PRACTICE:

By and large the efforts of the American Civil Liberties Union (ACLU), Planned Parenthood of America (PPA), other Feminist Groups, the National Organization for Women (NOW), the Gays, Lesbians, Bisexual and Transgender groups and different dissenting Christian groups like Call To Action, have steadily produced what can now be referred to as the "predominant secular culture" in America. This culture has across the board negative effects on organized religions. Moslems, Jews, Christians and others in America have in some way or another deviated from the original tenets of their religion because of some members' direct or indirect association with one or all of these groups. In my opinion, Christianity suffers most among the list of religions. Unfortunately a lot of Christians did not have good and sufficient catechetical training in Christianity. Since this brand of Christians is not grounded in the Faith, they are easily attracted to the worldly 'religion' preached by Hollywood and liberal America. They got their religious "thesis" not from Christ but from a misinterpreted "Freedom" in the First Amendment of the Constitution of the United States of America. Their kind of teaching is on a slippery slope because the First Amendment has been misread and Jesus and Christianity are bigger than any one nation no matter how big it is. Frankly speaking, their message is attractive to the flesh. Therefore the message, expressed in the media, movies and music, is popular. That explains why ACLU, PPA, NOW etc are very popular and powerful. The Catholic Archbishop of Denver highlights the state of affairs in question when he was speaking with "INSIDE THE VATICAN" Magazine. He said: "We're at a time for the Church in our Country when some Catholics – too many – are discovering that they've gradually become non-Catholics who happen to go to Mass."

(Most Rev. Charles Chaput, Archbishop of Denver.)

I'm sure the same can be said of other religions and major denominations of Christianity. We have witnessed an openly gay Episcopal priest being ordained a bishop. Just recently in California three of the four Episcopal priests running for the bishopric, are gay. The number of people leaving their brand of Christianity for another is growing fast for one or other of these reasons. The more the preacher goes soft on the Word of God, and goes heavy on platitudes, the more popular and more converts he or she gets. You can do the mathematics for the financial remuneration for the Church and the preacher. When numbers, money and the voice of what the people want detect what the preacher talks about or does not preach about, the goal of Christianity is lost. The Church ceases to be the Salt of the Earth and the Light of the World. When the Church can no longer give taste to a tasteless world and can no longer preserve the world from decay, as salt naturally does, there is no more need for the Church. When the Church can no longer shine on top of the hill to show people the Way and the Light, she should fold and close her doors. If the Church is no longer the city seated on a high mountain for all to see as a landmark, we don't need a Church anymore because one can argue that Christ, the Light of the world, is no longer the Head of that Church. Through misguided ministers of religion, the popular culture has taken over the role of leadership in churches. In some quarters, this has been the goal. If there is no God, no religion, no Church; there will be no conscience. Then humanism will take over and there will be no laws, no discipline, no right, no wrong; anything and everything becomes fair game. Can you imagine that kind of America? Yes, we are almost there and will arrive sooner than later unless there is a change of heart.

Why would a preacher deny Christ, the Head of the Church, to align with the world when Christ said that His followers live in the world but are not of the world? There could be a number of reasons:

Some priests, preachers and pastors have personal and self-serving agendas. That is to say they invited themselves to the party. Some even installed themselves and pick up a Bible. They were not invited by the Master. They take advantage of those people in the pews, who think they can and are willing to pay their way to Heaven. If the preacher is willing to tell them what they want to hear, they will give the preacher what he asks for. Consequently the desired goal is to obtain magic on the one hand and to make money off the people on the other. Everyone goes home "happy".

The next possible reason for a minister of religion to preach other than God's Word is that some preachers have little knowledge of the One they are supposed to serve. It is a fact that no one can give what one does not have. (Nemo dat quod non habet is a Latin adage.) The problem with the second group is ignorance. The One group of preachers has very likely put in a lot of individual studies or even got degrees for the same purpose like any other job but somewhere down the line in their ministry, they lost their faith like the seeds that fell on thorns. This group may have been swept off their feet by the prevailing culture. They become angry over the years with themselves, with God and start acting out maliciously; they make it a duty to "stick it to the man" by taking it out on their Master. This group of pastors gets some consolation in the claim of being supposedly "au-currant". If they are Catholic priests they say that they are in keeping with the "Spirit of Vatican Two". Fortunately a lot of the faithful are educated enough to read the Vatican 11 documents to see for themselves that these priests are out on the left field and are not teaching Vatican 11 at all. This last group, the ordained Catholic priest, is very dangerous because they are angry and are teaching out of malice and frustration. Being inside the Church and active, they still have a lot of cloud with the unsuspecting Parishioners. There are, however some parishioners, who want the easy way out. These will assist those priests to inflict more serious injuries to the Church. Over all there is enough ignorance to go round in the pews. For people of faith to be consumed by the predominant culture is not a sign of brilliance and good sense. If anything, it is a sign of a lack in good sense and good judgment.

In any religion, there are some things that are basic. In Christianity it should be pretty clear that the Church is not a democracy where the majority prevails. Some people erroneously or maliciously propound that the will of the people should be followed in the Church, whether the opinion is morally right or wrong. "We are the Church", they say. But this kind of concept is not in keeping with the nature of Church and religion. Man has never initiated a relation with God. It has always been God, who enters into the life of man. Man has only responded to God's initial move. It has never been man, who calls the shots in a relationship between him and God. Instead, without exception God calls the shots. He makes the rules and man obeys the rules. Whom did God consult before He created the world or man? Whom did He consult before He decided on the Ten Commandments? God created us and gave us those laws in love and asked us to obey them to reciprocate His love for us. As far as Divine Laws are concerned, we don't make laws; we obey them. That is why the nature of the Church is essentially hierarchical. It could not be democratic as some people want to make it. It does not come from ground up; it comes from above to us from historical times to the present. In a democracy, people assemble from the base, to elect people, who have a say in Government and in making laws. If it is not working, the people can go back and change them through another election. In religion, it is different. The Ten Commandments are still the same and will always be the same even though some progressives would like to change some. After all, they say, we are Americans and in the twenty first century. This mix-up is one of the problems facing us as Americans, who are trying to replace the hierarchical structure with the democratic structure. In a sense this is the genesis of our social and psychological problems in Church matters. The loss of the sense of the sacred is a direct result of this attempt to replace the Divine with the secular; the law of God with the law of man. Some have proposed that we come together to make our own laws because the law of God is too hard for modern man to obey. One can see this sentiment reflected in the Congress of the United States of America, the Supreme Court, various levels of Federal and State Courts, and different State Legislatures and Assemblies. If we cannot keep God's law, how can we maintain the rule of law made by man? Hence there will always be a struggle and conflict between the secular and the practice of religion. Fortunately or unfortunately they all revolve around the same man, who is secular and spiritually religious. Peace will continue to be illusive until all laws reflect their origin, God Himself.

RELIGIOUS DISSENT:

Looking at the nature and origin of religion, God's invitation and man's response, it becomes stupid and nonsensical for anyone to even envision religious dissent as a viable alternative. People dissent in opinions. But in God and religion, who is talking about opinion or consultation, for one to have room for dissent? As we saw earlier, God did not need our opinion to create the world or make the laws of nature or the laws man received on Mount Sinai. Why should an individual think that he is dissenting from the laws of God or the authoritative teachings of the Church, which has Jesus as its head? In the Catholic Church, for instance, there are some talks about dissenting priests or nuns against the teachings of the Church. What does that really mean? Some priests or nuns want to be in the Church of Christ and still run their own "show"? If one really knows the nature of religion, is that possible? The concept of dissent in the Church is equivalent to what is happening in the free speech concept of the First Amendment. Out of ignorance or fools hardiness, some people dissent from Church teachings and doctrines, even people who are supposed to know better. They can't seem to rise to the level of making a distinction between the American Constitution made by man and the Constitution made by God or the Leaders of the Church of Christ with Him as the Head.

In the American Catholic Church today, these are the main areas of dissent by some group of American Catholics: 1. Artificial Contraception, 2. Abortion, 3. Women ordination, 4. Gay rights and 5. Priestly Celibacy. We are discussing these issues because they are the results of an unfortunate misunderstanding of the relationship between the Church and State as enunciated above. We contend that there should be no conflict between the Church and State if God gets His rightful place in the affairs of man. Ignorantly or purposefully certain individuals in the Church have chosen to apply the civil, political standards on Church issues. In other words they are trying to super-impose the will of man on the will of God. And that makes all these dissents ridiculous.

1. Artificial Contraception: The Church is against artificial contraception because it is by its nature against God's design for procreation in the context of marriage and family. God put in place for married couples the spacing of the times to have children. In a given month every woman is capable of getting pregnant for only about four days. This is nature controlling birth. That means that for twenty something days a married couple can have sex without the woman getting pregnant guaranteed by nature. But for some people, who do not want to be responsible for anything, this is too much a task to follow some instruction. Everything must be at their time. The Billings Ovulation method of birth control is the natural family planning put in place by God. All that the couples need to do is be responsible, careful and patient. Instead of doing it God's way, some people, who advocate artificial birth control, would like to do it their way and now. Non married people like to join in on the "fun" too. For artificial contraception advocates, sex has ceased to be an expression of love between married men and their wives; instead it has become a causal recreational pastime among the unmarried, teens and adults. Two perfect strangers could meet in a bar one night, have sex never to see each other again. Artificial contraception helped to make a sacred act, a casual and an unholy act. Artificial contraception invited the devil into the bedrooms of married men and women. When the devil took over, he planted the seed of excessive divorce, carelessness and irresponsible behaviors that lead ultimately to abortion and other diseases. This is why the architects and the builders of Griswold v. Connecticut have the greater sin. We hope they did repent. For those Christians, who think they can dissent on artificial birth control, should think twice about the consequences of *stubbornly* disobeying Christ and his Church.

2. Abortion: We have devoted quite some time on this subject. But here we are looking at it from the vantage point of believers and Christians, who should know better all the evil connotations of killing an unborn baby. It is even far worse when Catholic Christians or Christians in general, who strongly believe in Roe v. Wade still profess to be active and practicing Catholics or Christians. They go so far as to proudly defend and campaign on abortion platform during elections. They actively support and vote for death instead of life. But on Sundays they will go to the Altar and receive Holy Communion. Of such people St. Paul gave this warning in 1Cor. 11: 23-29:

> "For I received from the Lord what I also handed on to you, that the Lord Jesus, on the night he was handed over, took bread and after he had given thanks, broke it and said: 'This is my body that is for you. Do this in remembrance of me. In the same way he took the cup after Supper, saying, 'This cup is the new covenant in my blood. Do this, as often as you drink it, in remembrance of me.' For as often as you eat this bread and drink the cup, you proclaim the death of the Lord until he comes. Therefore whoever eats the bread or drinks the cup of the Lord unworthily will have to answer for the body and blood of the Lord. A person should examine himself, and so eat the bread and drink the cup. For anyone who eats and drinks without discerning the body, eats and drinks judgment on himself."

This admonition of St. Paul should be an eye opener for those Catholics, who receive the Body and Blood of the Lord with impunity and reckless abandon as if to dare God to act. Whether priest or lay, it is a dangerous venture to support, abate or promote abortion, which Pope John Paul 11 called "the culture of death", or active gay-life style and continue to receive the body and Blood of Christ.

3. Gay rights: Some of the dissenters in the Catholic Church are gays, lesbians, bisexuals and trans-genders. That combination speaks a lot as to what is going on here – uninhibited behavior to be whatever you want any time – be heterosexual this week and gay next week because you can. It is almost like asking: who is God to determine whether I am a man or woman this week or next or even permanently? That is troubling, to say the least. In the last twenty or thirty years, this group has been making waves; but in the last ten to fifteen years, they have become a great political force in America. We are going to look at it only on the religious level. Homosexuality is a condition that is flawed according to the Scriptures just as any other sinful condition in man is flawed. The Catholic Church teaches that if one has an attraction toward people of ones own gender but does not act it out, that is to say, remains a celibate one is not committing any sin just as a man can have an attraction toward a woman and remain a celibate. But if one has sexual encounters with some one of the same sex it is gravely sinful on two levels. It is an unnatural act as well as a sinful act just as fornication or adultery is among heterosexual people if they are not husband and wife. The Catechism of the Catholic Church weighed in on the subject thus:

"Basing itself on Sacred Scriptures, which presents homosexual acts as acts of grave depravity, tradition has always declared that homosexual acts are intrinsically disordered. They are contrary to the natural law. They close the sexual act to the gift of life."

(Catechism of the Catholic Church: #2357)

Sometimes people say that it is unfair not to recognize and endorse sex between two men or two women. It is not unfair because the Church also condemns sexual encounters between a man and a woman outside of marriage. Such critics base their argument on the civil legislation, which allows or condones sex between two consenting man and woman. God's position is that any sexual acts outside of marriage are sinful. It is unfortunate that some priests do not seem to understand this teaching. In an article in INSIDE THE VATICAN Magazine, titled "Gay" Priest: An Oxymoron, John Mallon said: "Some (priests) even go so far as to claim their homosexuality is a "gift from God" or that God made me this way." (December2005 edition) To say that God made something "intrinsically evil" would be accusing God of the source of sin and evil. There are hundreds of thousands of Americans who are kleptomaniacs. These people have that tendency to steal things even when they don't need them. Some of them are rich people, who have no need of steal anything. Do they go about asking to be recognized to steal or evade prosecution? Have they formed a group to have a yearly kleptomaniacs' parade? They know that taking what does not belong to them, is wrong, natural tendency to steal or not, notwithstanding. They quietly struggle with their cross. A good number of them go for therapy and change or minimize the frequency. Many people who were gays went through some therapy and became normal. They have enough sense to know that God's law comes first. Some people are born blind or crippled. Are these abnormalities 'blessings' from God to write home about? People, who have no agenda, accept their handicaps and try to make the best of their situation by seeking whatever medical help there is on the market. Everyone, including the homosexual, has a cross in life to carry. To justify sickness or an abnormality as "blessing from God" is disingenuous and coming from a Catholic priest is over the top and does not help the condition.

The book of Genesis, chapter 19 gives an account of the destruction of Sodom and Gomorrah, two cities that were known for their sexual immorality for which God sent two angels in the form of men to destroy them. Lot, the brother of Abraham received these two men as his guests not knowing their mission or that they were angels of the Lord. Seeing them enter Lot's house, the people of Sodom came that evening to take them saying to Lot: "Where are the men who came to your house tonight? Bring them out to us that we may have intimacies with them." Lot hid them and came out to plead with them not to disrespect his guests. He told them: "I beg you, my brothers, not to do this wicked thing. I have two daughters who have never had intercourse with men. Let me bring them out to you, and you may do to them as you please." But they refused and forced their way into the house. Homosexual sin is also called sodomy after the city of Sodom. Until recently many States of the Republic had "Sodomy Laws" on their books. Now these laws are no longer "politically correct" and have been abrogated.

Writing about the sinfulness of homosexual activity St. Paul, in the New Testament, said: "Therefore, God handed them over to impurity through the lusts of their hearts for the mutual degradation of their bodies. They exchanged the truth of God for a lie and revered and worshipped the creature rather than the creator, who is blessed for ever. Amen. Therefore God handed them over to degrading passions. Their females exchanged natural relations for unnatural, and their males likewise gave up natural relations with females and burned with lust for one another. Males did shameful things with males and thus received in their own persons the due penalty for their perversity. And since they did not see fit to acknowledge God,

God handed them over to their undiscerning mind to do what is improper." Romans 1: 24-28.

It is interesting to note that God handed them over to degrading passions. This is because the people abandoned God, His authority and Commandments and became laws unto themselves as we in America and elsewhere have lately become our own lawgivers. God cut them loose and they woefully fell into disgraceful, unnatural and shameful acts. We see this scenario repeat itself many times in Scripture. We saw it in the Old Testament and New Testament. About divorce among the Israelites Jesus said that it was because of their hardness of heart that Moses allowed them divorce; divorce was not part of marriage from the beginning. As voters we ask our Representatives to give us laws that contravene God's laws.

The same disapproval of homosexual activity is also expressed in the Book of Leviticus: "If a man lies with a male as with a woman, both of them shall be put to death for their abominable deed." (Book of Leviticus. 20: 13.)

Referencing the sin of the city of Sodom in Genesis, the Apostle Paul wrote to Timothy: "We know that the law is good, provided that one uses it as law with the understanding that law is meant not for a righteous person but for the lawless and unruly, the godless and sinful, the unholy and profane, those who kill their fathers or mothers, murders, the unchaste, sodomites, kidnappers, liars perjurers and whatever else is opposed to sound teaching." (First Letter to Timothy 1: 8-10.)

This is what 1Cor.6: 9 had to say on the subject:

"Do you not know that the unjust will not inherit the kingdom of God? Do not be deceived; neither fornicators nor idolaters nor adulterers nor boy prostitutes nor **sodomites** nor thieves nor the greedy nor drunkards nor slanders nor robbers will inherit the kingdom of God."

"Likewise, Sodom and Gomorrah, and the surrounding towns, which, in the same manner as they, indulged in sexual promiscuity and practiced *unnatural vice*, serve as an example by undergoing a punishment of eternal fire." (Jude 1: 7.)

These are some of the reasons why the Church cannot condone the practice of homosexual acts or recognize homosexual marriages.

Dissent and Gay parades will not do anyone any good, physically or spiritually. No amount of political cloud by gay politicians and or priests will affect God's law. Some politicians and priests may use their official positions any way they want, the Word of God will win in the long run.

It may be appropriate to say a few things in this section regarding the priests' sexual scandal in the Catholic Church. It is unfortunate that it ever happened on the one hand and a blessing to the Catholic Church that it happened on the other. First of all, the National Media and a lot of liberals stretched the story. They loved it. They had a ball. It was like a pay back time for them. Every attempt was made to silence the moral conscience of the Nation. If they could succeed in killing the one voice of the Catholic Church, there would be no strong voice to call the attention of people to societal wrongs. They thought that with one down, the Evangelicals would be weak. If they could succeed in saying "healer, heal yourself first", they would no longer feel obligated to listen to the prophetic voice of the Church. That would have been a good point if the Church taught any error or condoned the mess. As it is, very stupid and serious mistakes were made by a very negligible number of priests. In as much as those were serious sins, the percentage was very, very small compared to the majority of very good priests in the Country. Our Lord and master had twelve Apostles and He lost one. We are by no means minimizing the gravity of the offence. Rather it was the sinister interest the liberal media had on the subject that elicited this comment.

On the other hand, it was a blessing for the Catholic Church as a whole that the scandal broke. It pointed the search light on a neglected issue, namely the moral decadence in the Church here for many years. Like the American government running away from God's laws, the American Catholic Church was drifting away from Rome and orthodoxy. Some bishops and priests were operating the Church under their care as private corporations. Some bishops assumed the role of Popes and pastors of churches elevated their parishes to mini dioceses with them as the mini-bishops. As it were, ecclesiastical law and order broke down. As far back as 1968, the Canadian Catholic Bishops collectively dissented from Pope Paul

VI's "Humanae Vitae", which was upholding the teaching of the Catholic Church against Artificial Birth Control in favor of "human life". In their response to the Pope's Encyclical the bishops claimed in contradiction to the Pope's document that "whoever honestly chooses that course (artificial birth control) which seems right to him does so in good conscience". In other words the faithful should not follow the teaching Authority of the Pope, but should follow their own conscience, informed or not. How is the conscience informed? It is through the teaching of the Church. That Episcopal endorsement from the bishops of our neighbors to the north armed a lot of other Catholics to dissent in all kinds of Church teachings in America. It acted as a license for theologians, priests, nuns and lay-people to challenge the Authority of the Pope and the Church. Since then many Catholics started to promote artificial birth control, abortions, sex outside marriage, divorce, pornography, and same sex marriage. Some Catholic hospitals did no longer see anything wrong with facilitating and performing abortions in their facilities.

Seminaries were no different from regular, secular universities. Many of the Catholic Universities were morally worse than some secular ones. University Presidents and Rectors of Major Seminaries openly dissented from Catholic teachings and doctrines. A Catholic educator in Ontario Province, Canada, Blaise Thompson refused to remove "The Catechism of the Catholic Church" from the reading list of his Catechism class and was fired by authorities. The Catholic Priesthood became a convenient refuge for gay men. But in some Catholic Universities "Feminist theology" made its way into the course list. A 36 year old unmarried man did not have to give any explanation about why he is single or why he is not seen in the company of women. No one would ask him why he does not date because he is a priest. He did no longer look out of place or awkward to be seen with boys all the time because as a celibate priest, he was not supposed to have girls that close. But unfortunately he is gay. The problem is that boys are to a gay priest what girls are to a heterosexual man who may be a sexual predator. This is how the gays infiltrated the Catholic Church and gave the Church in America a bad name just as gays infiltrated the Military, a situation that could cause some security breaches for the Military combat readiness. Under President

Clinton, the Congress adopted a "don't ask, don't tell" policy, which is still in force till today. It is like saying "sweep it under the rug"; don't tell us; we don't want to know. This was a compromise Bill by Congress to make Mr. Clinton withdraw an Executive order he signed the week he took office allowing openly gay people to serve in the Military contrary to an existing law banning gays in the Military because that could compromise security. That was what the priests' scandal did to the Church in America; it did compromise the integrity of the priests' relationship with young people.

But on a positive note, the scandal has opened the eyes of the Church authorities in the areas of Church doctrines, Personnel issues and Seminary training. Many Bishops have started to get into serious dialogue concerning abuses in the Liturgical practices among the so-called dissenting priests, flaws in the recruitment of seminarians and professors who teach in seminaries, an overhaul of priestly formation in a good number of Seminaries, the denial among some priests and laity concerning the Real Presence of Christ in the Holy Eucharist and abuses in a variety of other Sacraments like Confession, Marriage and issues about divorce and remarriage, etc. After Vatican 11, there was a general misconception that some of the essential laws and disciplines of the Catholic Church were dismantled or at least, relaxed. There was an overall poor Catechesis in the Country to prepare the people for Vatican11 implementation. That poor preparation created a kind of ecclesiastical free for all in the Church. Every one, who attended one or two seminars on the Liturgy or catechesis, became an expert on the Church. Newly baptized adults became experts on Vatican 11 documents because they went through R.C.I.A. Without reading the documents of Vatican 11, these so-called experts began to teach authoritatively what they think constitutes the Catholic doctrine and what does not. Musicians started to compose and launch music without ecclesiastical approval of lyrics and style of music. Priests started to experiment on all kinds of Liturgies without official Church sanction. Some priests, who were sitting on the fence, used the opportunity to do damage to the Church. The result was that many American Catholics became "non-Catholics" while still considering themselves Catholics. Some of the blame goes to the many lay people, some of who, were simply carried away and others who were looking for an opportunity to show that they were right in their desires. But most of the blame goes to the Church authorities for not implementing proper catechesis in their parishes and dioceses for whatever reason.

The generation of Catholics after Vatican 11 has a big void in the essence, meaning and practice of the Catholic Church. A good number of them made their First Holy Communion, Confirmation and some, the Sacrament of Matrimony and yet have never for once confessed their sins. Now they have children of their own to raise. What kind of children are they going to raise with that kind of background? Who dropped the ball on this issue? Some Pastors stopped the practice of First Confession before First Holy Communion because they said that children of First Communion age do neither know nor commit sin. Right! And that was the end of Confession in their lives. They went through Confirmation and marriage and the priests did not know because the priest again did a sloppy job. Unfortunately there are many such Catholics now all over the Country. That gap caused a lot of damage to the Catholic Church because the lack of a sense of sin in their lives has created a flawed Theology, which eventually affected the morality of the individual Catholics in particular and society at large. Unfortunately still some of these Catholics became priests. These and so many other cases led to some of what happened to the Church that we are dealing with now both in the scandal and elsewhere.

The priests' scandal became the "Felix culpa" (Oh happy fault) of our time. Since 2002 priests' scandal, the Church has been having a spiritual and internal auditing, which is producing good results. "Politically incorrect" things are now being said openly without any challenges from all kinds of quarters with the rank and file of the clergy. Many outspoken priests in favor of dissent in the Church were greatly silenced because persisting in their former posture would indorse the theology and other issues that created and nurtured the cause of the scandal. Thanks to the scandal itself! Many bishops not only have oversight committees to make sure there will be no more sex abuses, but to make sure that Seminaries are complying with the Catholic teaching. They now do everything in their power to see that holy and dedicated seminarians will no longer be disqualified from seminaries because they are "too conservative" or too popish or "pious" for the priesthood of the twentieth and twenty first centuries. For many years some seminary authorities have discouraged, intimidated or expelled good, sincere, prayerful and holy seminarians because they have either expressed dissatisfaction with the low moral standard in their seminary or they have enthusiastically supported the teachings of the Universal Church. An open support of the Holy Father, an expression of disgust for gay activities in the seminary could cause a seminarian to be "unfit" for the priesthood. It is sad and unfortunate and almost unimaginable that a man could be expelled from the seminary or harassed enough that he could decide to leave himself simply because he was doing what he was supposed to do as a good candidate for the priesthood. That is what happens when the enemy infiltrates the system and gets to the top of the power ladder. The way to kill the Church (if it were possible) would be to kill the priesthood – don't let good seminarians go through and put in as many bad ones as possible. If the Evil-one gets hold of one pastor, he has a stronghold on the entire parish. But now, as a result of the scandal, many of such practices in the Seminaries are at least minimized, since nobody wants to be associated with the scandal and its notoriety. Many dioceses have almost become bankrupt as a result of monetary pay outs. Many can no longer financially run their dioceses comfortably. Everybody is trying to do what the Church has always asked her priests to do: To preach the Good News when it is comfortable and when it is not, to teach what they believe and practice what they preach. The jury is still out on the outcome; but the prognosis is good. Many bishops have adopted a no tolerance for priestly dissent. The tolerance in the past was responsible for many bishops being on the hot seats for crimes they did not commit themselves. When very few priests went off the line through homosexual acting out, the individual bishops did not call them to order as the Canon Law prescribed. Instead they patched up the problem until the individual priests re-offended again and again. Now the affected dioceses are now paying for it heavily. Some are financially in red as a result. As I said earlier the moral decadence experienced in the Catholic Church was also experienced in other denominations of Christianity and religions. There were dissents all over in the Protestant denominations, for example. Many women groups lined up for ordinations and gays marriages were officially performed and recognized. The secular movement entered the Church. Church people in general abandoned the Bible teachings and aligned with Congress in deep seated religious matters which Congress had no competence in weighing in on.

4. Women ordination: Some women religious feminists and a few radical priests have been pressing for the ordination of women to the priesthood. All over the country, there are pockets of them, who have formed some groups like "call to action", a dissident organization "within" the Catholic Church whose mission is to push for women ordination, married priesthood and remarriage of divorced Catholics. They are capitalizing on the scarcity of priests in the Country to push for married priests and women ordination as a solution to the shortage of priests. Married Clergy and ordination of women will not solve the shortage of priests in the country. Moral laxity in the Church is primarily the cause of the shortage. Firstly many priests are no longer happy with their vocation. They cannot inspire or attract young people to the priesthood. Young people like challenge and there is little or none left in the priesthood as it is now. If there is no good reason for them to sacrifice a family of their own, it is not worth even trying. Many dioceses in America which run seminaries according to the Canon Law have their seminaries full. If going to a regular university is the same as going to the seminary, young people would choose going to the regular, secular university. Secondly the two child average per family in the Country now is not any help either. So the ordination of women, if it were to happen, would not solve the problem. Because of this move in some quarters, His Holiness, Pope John Paul 11, of happy memory, issued a statement in his 1994 letter – "Ordinatio sacerdotalis":

"In order that all doubt may be removed regarding a matter of great importance, a matter which pertains to the Church's divine constitution itself, in virtue of my ministry of confirming the brethren (cf. Luke 22: 32) I declare that the Church has no authority whatsoever to confer priestly ordination on women and that this judgment is to be definitively held by all the Church's faithful."

This is a definitive pronouncement from the Vicar of Christ on earth. "Roma locuta est, causa finita". End of the story!! Unfortunately some dissidents, priests, nuns and lay do not get it. They have relentlessly pursued a dead issue till today. There are a number of women parading as "priests" in the Catholic Church. Some claim to be ordained by dissident Bishops overseas on a boat in the international waters. That explains it. Just recently San Francisco FAITH, a Bay Area Lay Catholic Newspaper (June, 2006) carried an article by Christopher Zehnder, titled: <u>"Womanpriest" saying "Mass" at San Jose State</u>. It showed Victoria Rue, a Catholic, 'Comparative religious studies and women's studies' professor at San Jose State University dressed in an alb and stole presenting a loaf of bread. The article said that "a former Jesuit priest, who left the ministry to get married" was concelebrating with her. In an interview Rue was reported to say:

"The goals of our New Catholic Community are to reverence persons who seek authority and inclusion in the worship ceremony, who have experienced divorce and remarriage, who seek progressive exploration of ideas, who want imagination and daring, who are concerned deeply about God's creation and how to preserve it and who seek personal and spiritual integrity." Later in the interview, she told the Spartan Daily: "We are not trying to start a new Church; we are Roman Catholics."

Wha-o-o!! This is an interesting piece. Ms Rue and her group do not want to start another Church but they want to reverence persons who seek authority and inclusion in the worship ceremony. They are Roman Catholics who do not obey the Pope. Isn't that interesting? They do not want to start another Church but they are willing to disobey the Vicar of Christ on earth. Who knows why they still want to be called Roman Catholic? Could it be that they need a name to ride on? Or could it be that not many people would be interested in their brand of Christianity if they don't retain the name "Roman Catholic"? Obviously it is not love for the Church as love of Ms Rue's ego and power as in "to reverence persons who seek authority". I would not be surprised if Ms Rue is divorced and perhaps remarried without an annulment. The high volume of divorce in the United States is as a result of the general moral laxity, arrogance and mentality of so-called Catholics like Ms Rue. Statistics show that in

1993, out of 64, 437 cases of annulments, the United States alone accounts for 44,000 cases. But in 1968 only 338 annulments were granted in the United States of America. It is estimated that there are about 8 million American Catholics, who are divorced. Ms Rue has potential Church members in the 8million divorced Americans.

It is understandable to see that a former Jesuit priest, who left the priesthood to get married, is in on the bizarre story about a "wana be woman priest"; but it is not funny to read the comment of an active Catholic priest on the subject of the ordination of women in the Catholic Church when His Holiness Pope John Paul 11 had made a definitive pronouncement on the subject. That is one example of dissent. At least the former Jesuit priest had the courage to leave the priesthood in order to get married. The very reverend Father Jose Rubio, the San Jose State campus ministry's Chaplain, according to the *Spartan Daily,* "believes that the Catholic people are not ready yet for this change..." The paper said that Fr. Rubio added that it will happen whenever everybody is ready to accept it. He went on: "It is a starting movement, and I think it is something whose time is not there yet. It is something that will happen in the future." As a campus ministry Chaplain Fr. Rubio seems to have endorsed this dissident and Protesting group when he said: "But sometimes the spirit calls people to do new things in new ways...I think things have to happen because people want it." By leaving the ordination of women open, Fr. Rubio has exposed his ignorance of the Catholic Church structure; that it is not a democracy where the "Catholic people" will come together and decide that it is time now to ordain women in the Catholic Church. It is not a State Government where people vote from ground up to form a representative Government. The Church is an establishment at God's instance in a hierarchical manner. We did not come together to form a Church, as in a Government; we did not go to God; God came to us. One would have thought that Fr. Rubio and other priests, who think like him, have read about De Ecclesia (concerning the Church) in the Seminary and stop embarrassing the Church and Seminary education. It is a sorry situation and time when a Catholic priest openly declares that he thinks that "things have to happen because people want it." How many other things are out there that people want and can't because they are not what

God wants? What if he knew the full implication of that statement! I think that Bishops should insist that a solid Philosophy degree should be a 'conditio sine qua non' for ordination to the priesthood in the United States of America. That will help people like Fr. Rubio to reason well.

5. Celibacy: When people hear about celibacy, they only think of the celibacy of priests and religious in the Catholic Church. In a sense it is a good thing to think like that. But that is not the full picture. All lay people, married and unmarried are called to celibacy too. Sexual faithfulness for single and married people is a part of God's covenant with his people. For a single person it involves being chaste until he or she gets married. It is not an option; it is a requirement from Jesus. For a married person it involves a contractual agreement of sex with only one partner within the context of marriage. But for a priest or religious, it involves a chaste life with a vow to remain so permanently. This vow enhances the dignity of the special call of the priesthood and religious life. It is not meant for all. This kind of celibacy is a calling. According to Scriptures, some were born eunuchs from birth; some were made eunuchs by other people either willingly or unwillingly and some became eunuchs for the kingdom of heaven by choice. Religious Celibates became eunuchs for the kingdom of heaven. They are not stupid as some people think. Look at it this way: Celibates in the Catholic Church are like the man in Jesus' parable of 'the hidden treasure', which a man found in the ground. He reburied it and went home, sold all he had to buy the land. Why? It was because he knew that the value of the treasure is beyond anything he could imagine. Would you say he is dumb to sell all he had? No way!! Of course, for anyone who does not understand the value of what he found, he would appear to be stupid selling all he had to buy the land. But, in fact, he is very smart and forward looking. All those, who made themselves eunuchs for the kingdom of God, are very smart and courageous people. The same thing is applicable to all those single people who remain celibates until they marry and those married couples who remain celibates within marriage. It is, of course, a sacrifice on the part of all celibates for a higher goal. But unfortunately ignorance of this fact makes some people, priest and lay alike, to ask for the abolition of celibacy among priests and religious in the Catholic Church in favor of married clergy and religious. If only they knew the implications of such a demand! The marriage of the Catholic clergy, like the ordination of women, would not add any enhancement to the Catholic Church as it is. On the contrary, the existence of celibacy in the Catholic Church in the West has enhanced the Church just as it did in the lives of St. Paul and St. John, hermits, monks and many other saints in the previous centuries of the Church.

When people call for the marriage of priests and religious in the American Catholic Church lately, what is their motivation? Is it for the good of the Church, the spiritual wellbeing of the individuals concerned or just to contradict the Church in order to conform to the world? This is one way to weaken the Catholic Church by chipping the pillars down one by one. For we already know that clerical celibacy has nothing to do with the priests who, in our recent history, molested young boys. Those people, who molest children, are suffering from a serious disease. If anyone is in doubt, let them watch any "Gay/Lesbian Parade" to see handsome and beautiful men and women, who are not under any priestly or religious celibacy laws. It is also on record that molestation of young boys has manifested itself among married men, including Protestant clergymen, who are married. So who is going to benefit from the call for Catholic Clergy marriage and who is pushing it? Surely it is neither the Pope nor Church Authorities. We also know that this continuous call is not for the good of the Church and not for the spiritual welfare of the priests and religious. It is for those who want to score a point by trying to weaken the foundation of the Church. Clerical celibacy benefits the Church and participating individuals too just as fasting and abstinence benefit individuals spiritually and edifies the Church collectively. Therefore the call must have a sinister motive especially when it comes from lay people, who are themselves free to marry and few disgruntled members of the clergy, who have no courage to leave the priesthood. For one thing, the few priests and nuns calling for clergy marriage are angry at the Church. Selfishness and arrogance push some to think that the rules of the game must be changed because they said so. One can securely conclude that there are a relentless group of people, who would like to destroy the Catholic priesthood because the success and holiness of the Catholic clergy pricks their conscience since evil likes company. The sacramental life of the Church is the life-source of the Church. It is through the sacraments that Christ feeds his Church. But without the Catholic priesthood, there are no Sacraments through which Christ, the Head, feeds His Church and "touches base" with His children. So it is a very sinister but smart move to start the attack from the priesthood. Some of the priests have lost their faith in the Church and the Sacraments. Administration of the Sacraments for this group of priests has become routine in which there is a livelihood, the only reason to hang on. The Bishop's admonition on the day they were ordained lost its meaning: namely *to preach what they believe, and practice what they preach*. Among those, some had the courage to leave the priesthood. But tragically there are still some who won't leave and they won't teach "the mind of the Church". That is a far worse damage to the Church because they are within the church; they represent the Church, which they don't believe in anymore. In some parishes a good number of people do not know any better. So whatever spiritual poison they get from such priests is what they as parents will hand on to their own children. Like cancer it spreads from parents to children to children's children. After a few decades, the Church will inherit a big number of nominal Catholics but practicing Protestants, who do not believe in the Sacrament of Confession or the Real Presence in the Eucharist, to mention just two. That will be the disastrous result of just one dissenting priest running a parish. Apart from the naively unsuspecting Parishioners who are mislead, there are some who know better but knowingly and willingly like to "enjoy the ride" with the Pastor, hoping that because he is the Pastor, who is an expert, they themselves would be set free from blame. It does not happen like that because they will be convicted by their own conscience.

In the Protestant denominations of the Christian Faith, we have the ugly head of dissent sticking out too. Dissent is the principal reason of fragmentations we see in the Protestant denominations. The only thing new is that the number and frequency of dissent and groups have increased. While the Catholic denomination is fairly in tact, Protestant denominations have been seriously wounded and fractured thousands of times. Except for a very few segments of the Protestant groups, which have some uniform structure of rituals and worship, the rest take the form which the one individual leader wants without reference to any other authority because "the buck stops with him". Invariably thousands of Protestant denominations have as many different and unique rites and rituals as there are individuals in them. Every group was a dissenter from the preceding one. In each case, there is an inter-play of egos of individuals which end ultimately in splits, divisions, and formation of new groups. The question is: Whose will is done in religion, God's or the leaders' or preachers'? Is disintegration the will of Christ, the Founder or man's will? If it is the will of God, why would Christ pray "that they may be one just as we are one" John 17: 11. (ut unum sint)? "I have other sheep that do not belong to this fold," Christ said. "These I must also lead and they will hear my voice, and there will be one flock, and one shepherd." (John. 10:16)

Why did Christ pray that they be "one flock and one shepherd"? The manifestation of egos and multiplication of churches are obviously not the way to fulfill God's prayer for His Church. The majority of the dissenting churches use only the Bible. Some strictly teach that there is no church or any need for one because Christ sent His Apostles to preach the Word. But they forget that Jesus established the Church, which in turn gave us the bible many years after Jesus had gone back to Heaven. The Apostles were functioning as a Church before the Bible was written. The assumption of authority to interpret the Bible at will is hardly the way to fulfill the message of Scripture or keep the Church of Christ intact. Once again dissent from any angle one looks at it, is not the will of Christ, the Founder and Head, who founded one Church, one baptism and one faith. Instead obedience is the only way to follow Christ, who came "to do the will of Him that sent me." Dissent can only weaken not strengthen the Church. Dissenters are borrowing from the secular, democratic world. The Evil One is making good use of the principle of "divide and conquer" to destroy the Church. But God forbid!

Religious dissent has many faces. It has the face of pride and ego; (Non serviam – I will not serve) it has the monetary, wealth and status face as well. Whenever these elements enter into religious practice, the devil is at his best. The mission of the Church changes immediately. The work, the message and its focus are no longer on Christ. People start preaching themselves and their egos, affluence and financial status flourish. Very soon after, greed, envy, and jealousy are nurtured inside the church breeding other dissents. Infighting is the next thing in line. Then the Word of God becomes the pun in their midst. Ecclesiastical divorces take place and each person defines his own "Christ" and his own church. After a number of "Praise the Lord," and "Alleluias", personality issues will play back all over again. These phenomena are responsible for members of Christ's body very much divided in many moral issues. If they all profess one and the same Jesus Christ, why would there be divisions in moral issues? We have an actively and openly gay bishop in the Episcopal Church, several active gay ministers in Catholic and Protestant Churches who are 'Gay and Proud'; some celebrate or go to "Dignity Mass"; there are some followers of Christ who are proud to be gay and anti 'Pro Life' issues and candidates in the political arena; there are millions who take contraceptives to block the possibility of a new child being born in this world; there are those believers in Christianity, who believe that they have a right to take away their own lives or those of others with their permission. Let us repeat St. Paul's question: is Christ divided? Some people think it is a way of being progressive and current. But Christ is *Progress* itself. Yet it is the same Christ *today*, the same Christ *yesterday* and the same Christ *tomorrow*. For these people morality is relative to persons and times. The same goes for the truth. There is no objective truth which is eternal for them. All such religions, which teach such ideologies, are only there for show or money or both. Religion should not be always pleasing to the people. By any means should religion only tell people what they want to hear? Should followers of Christ carry their cross daily and follow Jesus or would that upset people?

The Catholic Church has suffered a lot of bruises in the last thirty or forty years. Some of the minor injuries are from without but most of them come from within; and that is a shame, to put it mildly. The bruises were intended to be deep and devastating to the Body. But we are blessed that Christ Himself is the Head of that Church and has fortified Her with the promise that the gates of hell would not prevail against the Church. In spite of Christ's promise, some so-called Catholics go about defining their own idea of what the Church of Christ should be in the twenty first century. They deliberately flout Church teachings and go about fishing for any priests that would tell them what they want to hear, not what the Church of Christ teaches for all to believe on the mandate Christ gave to Peter and his Confreres. If they don't find the priests whose homilies would not prick their guilty conscience in their city or neighboring cities, they would look for another priest elsewhere or finally to a Protestant Minister, who would. They would join and become big donors as well as active Christians in that Church with the hope that their big donations and activity in a Protesting Church would make up for any deficiencies in their lives before. Many of these people don't listen to the Church; instead they listen to the prevailing culture which tells them they can marry as many times as they want and divorce as many times as they want. That was what pushed King Henry V111, a former Catholic King, to establish the Church of England (Anglican Church). They look at the Church as a democracy, where everything is determined by numbers and public opinion. As we saw earlier, that is far from what Christ wanted His Church to be. Even as democratic as groups, societies and clubs are, individual members don't come in and change rules in the middle of the game just because such changes would favor them. But some Catholics would like to marry and divorce, then remarry and still want to receive the Sacraments. Gay Catholics would want the rules about marriage and the reception of Holy Communion to change just because they want them to change. If the Church defends her position in these areas, these individuals would call the Church arrogant and insensitive. The Church in America has unfortunately taken the footsteps of the American political culture, where everybody has practically a right to do anything and everything. If anything goes wrong in so doing, the individuals would blame the Government for everything. Many times the individual does not accept responsibility or accountability for his actions. If he engages in risky behaviors and gets hurt, the Government takes the blame. In the same frame of mind, when people commit sins, instead of acknowledging that they have sinned and ask for forgiveness, they want to change the rules of the Church to accommodate them or else the Church is termed "insensitive and unforgiving". How can anyone forgive someone, who is intransigent and defying? These behaviors, either from a political or church perspective, have the same effect on the family, children and society. They marginalize God and Church; they perpetuate indiscipline, promiscuity, crime and violence in society.

What is responsible for the fracture in the American Catholic Church? Why do we have a sizeable portion of the Church – clergy and laity – in a dissenting mode? Some think that the origin of dissent in the Church is from the laity while some think that it came from the clergy. I tend to agree with the latter. As the Minor Seminaries were shut down, the nature and caliber of candidates for the Priesthood in the Catholic Church changed. College students became the major candidates for the priesthood in the Catholic Church. But the problem was that these men have been formed and shaped; some have their own agenda already; some were running into the Catholic priesthood for shelter. Almost all of them had little or no training in Latin, the official language of the Church. Very few of these men had enough time to learn about the Church and her culture and tradition; a good number had deep rooted affiliations in other Christian denominations. For the most part, many of these men were products of the sixties and their mindset is in words like "change", "progressive", "love", "earth religion"... The Liturgy for them is what you make up as "the Spirit" moves the individual priest and choir director. Self expression and individual interpretation became normal in the American Church. When the Vatican 11 was implemented, these manifestations were carried to another level. Thus dissent became entrenched. When some of these priests were made Bishops, dissent was enthroned in some dioceses in the United States of America through the endorsement of the diocesan bishop. Since the Church has no police, no army, how does one discipline a bishop or a priest? Some Bishops become "popes" in their dioceses and many Pastors of Churches considered themselves "bishops" of their parishes. They do not take any directive from their bishop. From the clerical arena and Church Sanctuary, dissent came down to the people in the pews. Like in the Protestant Churches and political parties, much of the Catholic Church in America has become democratic institutions. The people now want laws, rules and regulations to pass from the people up to God. If God doesn't like what the people have decided, tough!

It is lack of authority or the exercise thereof, and intransigence, which have landed the Church in America in the mess it finds itself today. Authorities, from Rome to America, got a wake up call with the scandal. The call came from God. Just as He did to the Israelites of old when they disobeyed him and followed other gods, God disgraced the Church to get the attention of the clergy and people. Just as the Lord let the Pagans defeat, humiliate and give orders to the people of God of old, He also gave the Church in America over to Civil Authorities and the media to judge and humiliate her. In so doing the Church goes through some kind of exile experience.

In a lot of ways, the American Church is longing for home, thanks to the scandal and the subsequent humiliation. But she will be allowed to return from "Babylon" and once more settle in her home in obedience to the Lord. The process has begun already. Just recently His Holiness Pope Benedict XV1 summoned a Synod of Bishops to Rome to re-establish our faith in the Eucharist and the proper way to celebrate the Liturgy according to Vatican 11. The Bishops looked into how and why there were abuses in the understanding of the Eucharist and the way to celebrate the Sacraments properly. The Synod Fathers, as they are called, identified where "we dropped the ball". They discovered that many priests did not celebrate the Holy Eucharist with due respect and devotion. That gave the people a reason to lose their faith in the Real Presence of Christ in the Eucharist. They pointed out that some priests do not have faith in the Sacraments they celebrate. These problems started with the end of Vatican 11. The timing coincided with the turbulent sixties in the United States. Is there a problem with Vatican 11 or did the people take liberty to implement the documents of Vatican 11 the way they wanted? Since dissent is not universal, the problem is not with the Vatican 11 Documents but with the implementation in some quarters. Dissent, defiance, intransigence, unrepentant and unyielding attitude will not lead to God; they lead away from God. The Synod Fathers made some 50 propositions or recommendations and put some into practice during the Synod. For the three weeks of the Synod, the participants had a one hour Eucharistic Adoration in the morning and one in the afternoon. On October 17, 2005, the Holy Father himself led the Holy hour in St. Peter's Basilica. With the help of some appointed Synod Fathers, the Pope will use the 50 propositions of the Synod to produce the post-synodal apostolic exhortation. That is a good sign of hope and return from "Babylon" for all the people of God.

Other Protestant Christian denominations are not free from this dangerous current. A lot of their members go to this or that particular Church because this or that Pastor tells them what they want to hear also. They are very ready to switch Churches to hear not the Word of God but what makes them "feel good". The Word of God is then reduced to mere "feelings". That is how we lost objective truth and a vast majority of Church-going Christians, Catholic and Protestant, hung unto "subjective truth", which we have treated extensively already. Once again the society is worse for it. It makes everybody right and nobody wrong. Every one becomes a god unto himself running around in a little heaven of his own. But we know for sure that everyone running around is not perfect and that this place is not heaven, by any means. Is there any wonder then that people have lost a sense of sin and the sense of the Sacred as well? Is there any surprise that young people or adults, for that matter, do not see anything wrong in sex outside of marriage, divorce and remarriage several times, the killing of unborn babies? It is this subjective attitude to the Truth which is responsible for more and more people doing things contrary to God's laws and feeling normal and comfortable about it because they "subjectively" think that it is fine for them.

CHAPTER EIGHT:
DISSENT IN THE NIGERIAN CHURCH?

The influence of media and other forms of communication technology have helped to make the world so small and compact that information flows across Continents in a matter of minutes. For practical purposes, many religions have become universal religions for the same reason. A Tele-Evangelist in Los Angeles could be seen all over the world at the same time. Whatever goes on in the American Church today is either read on the internet or seen on television in Nigeria almost immediately. Added to that is the fact that there are many Nigerians living in the United States of America. Lately Americans have started to frequent Nigeria too. Consequently there is a free flow of information to and from Nigeria. For various reasons many Nigerians, who were devout and practicing Christians in Nigeria before coming to America, rarely go to Church in the United States of America. Some claim that "the white-man", who brought Christianity to them in Nigeria, does not go to Church himself here in America. Of course that is not an accurate statement. It is based on the ignorance of people, who are looking for a justification for their mistakes. As shallow and lame as that excuse is, it is sufficient for them to relinquish their Faith. It does not end there; they carry the news home and make a few converts of their own. It only takes one individual to start the ball rolling. There is another group of Nigerians, which believes that, because Americans tend to ask why for almost everything, they also want to know the why of every religious issue. This group of Nigerians thinks that it is a sign of education to question even God Himself. Sooner or later they lose their faith because the object of religion deals, not with what is provable, but primarily with Mysteries that man will never understand or be able to explain fully. The third group of Nigerians is made up of those, who work and go to school seven days a week. They have no time for God, no time to go to Church or introduce their children to God or Church. If and when they go home to Nigeria, they would try to introduce the non-religious culture into the Nigerian society. It is, therefore, normal and fair to assume that religious dissent may also exist in the Nigerian Church as a result of these and other influences. There are probably more than one thousand different and independent Protestant denominations in Nigeria now. In major cities almost every block has a couple of these churches at close proximity. Earlier we have established that the multiplication of these churches is a sign of dissent itself and many of these Churches originated from the United States of America. Unlike these churches, every Catholic Church has a link and affiliation with the Church in Rome. The Protestant denominations do not have that kind of structure. Consequently starting a Church of this nature is not difficult.

There is dissent, and there is dissent. The Catholic Church in Nigeria is not facing the kind of dissent that we see in America, thank God. Like other American problems we don't know how much longer Nigeria will enjoy this Church peace and harmony. Some think it is a matter of time. The momentum of the pendulum might weaken before these morally challenging problems reach the Nigerian shores. What would the scenario look like were they to take root in Nigeria? There is no doubt that some kind of dissent has already infiltrated into the Catholic Church in Nigeria. But how fertile and welcoming would the moral land and atmosphere look like? Would the Nigerian Church welcome artificial contraception, abortion, gay life-style, women ordination and priestly marriage? There are all kinds of anomalies and evil things in people's minds always. But they don't become acceptable because some of the people voice their intentions. People always think murder, adultery, theft, rape arson. These are still against the law. The New York Times

International of Sunday 18th December, 2005 carried an article by Lydia Polgreen titled: "Nigerian Anglicans Seeing Gay Challenge to Orthodoxy". The subheading says: *The Nigerian Anglican Church objects to efforts to accommodate homosexuality*. One Mr. Davis Mac-Iyalla, who founded a group 'Changing Attitude Nigeria' told the reporter: "We want to tell the bishop that it is our church, too." He claimed to have hundreds of members. But the Anglican Church does not think that one can be a practicing homosexual and be a practicing Anglican too. "It cannot be supported by Scripture, it is against reason", said the Anglican Archbishop Akinola. "It is against nature. So we in the global south stand against it." Another Anglican from Port Harcourt said, "Homosexuality is a Western thing. In Nigeria we don't condone it, we don't tolerate it." According to the Times, gay men are often arrested and jailed up to 14 years because there is a Nigerian criminal code that bans acts "against the order of nature". In areas of Nigeria that adhere to Islamic law, the Shariah, the paper said the sentence for homosexual acts is death. It can be seen that the gays and lesbians in America are working their way to Nigeria. But the success will depend on the ground that the gay seed falls on. The Anglicans in the United States have caved in. But those in Nigeria have not. The senior specialist for Africa at the International Gay and Lesbian Human Rights Commission, Cary Alan Johnson thinks it is a global movement that should be given free reign. "There is a growth in identity-based movements, and there is an impact of the global gay identity where people throughout the world are seeing themselves as part of a larger global movement," he said. There is an argument that it is time; it is accepted elsewhere; things have changed. But the secretary general of the Anglican Church of Nigeria does not think that the gay issue is one about time. "The Bible and the creeds don't lend themselves to any variation over time." Oluranti Odubogun said. "They don't subject themselves to cultural changes. They are guidance given for human existence from age to age." It is still too early to make an intelligent forecast on all these issues. However, it seems that all the moral problems here in the United States of America are some how in Nigeria already but in camera for some. In the Catholic Church in Nigeria, there has not been any open discussion about any of the issues probably because the Catholic Church has not been as democratic as the Anglicans from the beginning. There are of course, many priests and nuns from Nigeria, who come to do advanced studies in the United States and go back to teach or work. We have no reason to think that any such trend is going to develop in the Nigerian Catholic Church. The only thing one can say with some moral certitude is that it is very unlikely that the moral relativity which exists in America now will gain a strong foothold in Nigeria. One can risk that conclusion because the people will not welcome any crazy ideas that are easily acceptable in America because of the culture of the people. Furthermore there is a unique coexistence between all the Christian denominations and Moslems in Nigeria when it comes to issues of abortion and gay marriage. Thank God, the Traditional Religionists, Moslems and Christians are all very strong in their Faith in those areas and are united against these weird American household issues that have been promoted in the guise of "Civil Rights" and "Individual Rights". Seeing what moral depravity has done to parts of Europe and currently in the U. S. A., the Nigerian people will be or rather should be extremely cautious in embracing these proven moral maladies condemned in the Old and New Testaments and books of other major Religions of the world. There are parts of Europe where the average number of children in a family is in fractions. Weird--eh? The gay culture and free, irresponsible sex, for instance, have decimated their population to the extent that in just a few more years, there may be scarcely anybody living there. While it is true that Nigerians have heavily borrowed a lot from America, their love and respect for family, children and life in general, are too core in their lives to be abandoned for these foreign behaviors, which are in themselves against everything they value and cherish. This is the background under which the Catholic Church in Nigeria draws her strength to combat dissent in the Church. The culture, as we discussed before, is too strong to be eroded by the new age, foreign influence especially when it touches on morality. One of the reasons for this write-up is to keep the Nigerian people posted about the impending danger, which, if left unchecked, will sneak in like cancer. Once in, it is very difficult to eradicate. Some African countries, where Americans frequent for vacations, have become victims already of low moral standards and aids. America is a living witness to the difficulty of going back to her moral glories of the past, when parents ran the household, loved their children (*uninhibited by smoking, alcohol and drugs*), took moral upbringing of their children seriously; when children loved and respected their parents and parents rejoiced and thanked God for every conception of a baby; when people did not have to lock their cars or houses for fear of break-ins, and children were the responsibility and joy of everybody in the neighborhood; when men had utmost respect for women (*and not mere sex objects*), protected them with their own lives and men were happy to be men and women, women, and marriage was naturally between a man and a woman and marriage was "until death do us part"; when the word gay was existent only in the dictionary and meant 'happy and outgoing'; when drug was only what the doctor prescribed for patients to make them well and Sunday was a Holy Day reserved for the Lord as in "the Lord's Day", and rest day was for family and friends; we are talking about the glorious days when people went to church as a family and really worshipped for hours and were happy doing it. Nigerians are not in a hurry about leaving the House of God. They are not in a hurry when they are worshipping God. They celebrate and in a celebration, people do not look at the watch because they are having a good time with the Lord. America has lost the sense of family to a great extent; Nigeria has not. When families celebrate with the family patriarch or matriarch surrounded by children, grand children and great grand children, no one is in a hurry. One could sincerely say: "La vie est belle." Thanks to God!

The average Nigerian family has about six or seven children. Many Americans, especially the women, do not think that having a big family is a good thing. That prospect alone can make the American woman sick. Priority! Some would say: "pregnant seven times?" It sounds impossible to most American women since the sixties, even though there are still some (very few) women in America today who have five, six or seven children. Before everybody's eyes, these families of five or more children raise them to be well-behaved, well educated Americans. The principle of success is the same in Nigeria as in America. There are a lot of advantages in big families. It reduces selfishness and narrow-mindedness, which is common in families of one or two children. People raised in big families learn to get along and share whatever they have with siblings and others later in life. Their bond of love is strong and intense. They develop a healthy sense of competition and drive. There is of course no boredom, intolerance or depression and loneliness because there is a lot to do and think about. Children in big families know how to look after each other. They set their priorities straight, not wasteful because there isn't enough to go round all the time. They children are survivors. All these are good recipe for God to come into the family. If they are Catholic, there is enough room for one or two to devote their lives for the spread of the Gospel in the Catholic priesthood or religious life. It is on that big family concept that Ireland spread the Catholic Church all over the world. The United States was one of the biggest beneficiaries of the generosity of the Irish Catholic families. Nigeria is another one through the Irish Holy Ghost priests, who sowed the seed of Catholicism in the South-eastern Nigeria, which now has the largest Catholic seminaries in the world. Big families played a very big role in America in the past as it has continued to play in Nigeria till date in spite of Western foreign culture. Our prayer is that it continues. Unfortunately the future of the Catholic Church in Ireland today is very bleak because they seem to have lost their faith or perhaps they have been converted by American world view. This is the crux of the point of this book. See where it has landed the Church in Ireland today. Now they don't have enough priests for their home mission; a big percentage of them do not go to Mass on Sundays anymore; they have started toying with contraception and abortion; moral decadence has set in with all its associates. Little by little, one thing leads to another. Dissent is born in the local Church among clergy and laypeople. America is played over again. If time is not taken to hold fast to the momentum in Nigeria, where the priests and clergy are very strong now, Nigeria could easily experience what happened to Europe and America.

At the promulgation of the documents of Vatican11 in 1965, the Nigerian was in the middle of unrest, which led to Military coups, a terrible crude war and a devastation of the almost three year war that claimed thousands of lives. The Church was seriously affected because the people were affected. The expatriate priests were forcefully repatriated to their home countries because they helped to bring relief to the suffering people of Biafra. That was the "sin" they committed. But in spite of all the hardship at the time, the Catholic Church in Nigeria started the work of implementation of Vatican 11 without questions asked. Necessary adaptations were carried out. There was a Liturgical Commission in every diocese of the Federation of Nigeria. Parish Councils and Pastoral Councils were set up in every parish and diocese in the Nation. After forty one years there are still parishes and dioceses in America that do not have parish councils and pastoral councils in place because some priests and bishops run the Church as private corporations. They do not take orders from Rome. In Nigeria musicians were encouraged to compose music with approved lyrics. Only ecclesiastical authorities approved both music and lyrics used in the liturgical celebrations. Both the Clergy and the Lay people assumed their new roles with out any deliberate abuses or dissent till date. The Local Churches are solidly in union with the Universal Church.

The natural and cultural love of children and family notwithstanding, the Nigerian clergy fully understood and accepted celibacy as the universal discipline of the Church in the West. It is understood that being a priest in the Church of the West, carries with it the gift of celibacy as a requirement. Dissent on that issue becomes childish. Closely related to that issue is the ordination of women. Again Nigerian women are smart enough to know that the Church is not a democracy; that there are rules in the Catholic Church as there are rules in every organization. The Nigerian Catholic women also know that they are the faith pillars of the Church, which begins in the family. They fully understand that they run the homes and have a great influence on the children of every family. The Catholic Women Organization (CWO) and the Mary League Girls are very strong arms of the Catholic Church in Nigeria. The Christian mothers are the first teachers of their children in the Catholic Faith. Nigerian Catholic women know that they don't play second fiddle in the Catholic Church. They are smart enough to know their roles in the Church and play it well and the Nigerian Church is better for it unlike some disgruntled, frustrated and unhappy women in American Catholic Church who want to be priests but do not have a clue what their roles and duties to their children and family are.

These "wa-na be priests" do neither have the spirit of the Church nor do they know the meaning of obedience in the Church; the spirit of revolution and dissent are all they know. The Nigerian Catholic women are well ahead of them in the knowledge and execution of Church laws and their practice.

The relationship between the priests and the bishops is cordial. Some times some priests may have issues with their bishops. Those are always treated on a personal level. Benefit of the doubt is given to the Church or the integrity of the office. The Canon Law guides the relationships between the priests and their bishop on the one hand, and the people and the clergy on the other. The Canon Law clearly defines the duties and obligations of each group. The hierarchical structure of the Church is well understood by all the parties. That is why there is no need for dissent. Dissent is the product of ignorance and pride. When the bishop respects and loves his priests, there is a better working relationship between them. He encourages and congratulates them when they do well and reprimands or punishes them according to Canon Law, when they make mistakes or go astray. As the bishop of a diocese, it is one of his duties to be a father to all his priests in every way. In Nigeria bishops don't run the dioceses by feelings. They follow the laws of the Church for the interest of the Church and the people of God in general even when that may upset a particular priest. That eventually will guide him back into the fold and in compliance.

The priests, in turn, respect and relate to the bishop as their spiritual father. The parishioners regard their priests as spiritual fathers and the priests love and treat them as their spiritual-God children as directed by Canon Law. When all hands are on deck, the bishop, clergy and the laity, and everyone is on the same page on the spiritual guidance from Rome, the Canon Law and the New Catechism, God's work is enhanced. Vocation becomes the fruit. In this kind of atmosphere, Evangelism is smooth and at the same time solid because everybody is reading from the same script and the "old man ego", which is always present, is at the rear, but powerless. Nobody is looking to be somebody else because each person is satisfied with who God called them to be in the service of Him. The fear of the United States' relationship with the Nigerian society is that the harmony in the Nigerian Church may be fractured. Some people in the American Church do not know who they are, and what it is that God has called them to be or do. This has come about for various reasons. But the effects are ugly and are manifested in weird personality traits and personality clashes, in religious dissent and political leanings. This is not what Nigeria needs at this time. Any assimilation of this aspect of American culture will only set back some inroads that the young indigenous Church has made in Nigeria in the last thirty something years since the end of the civil war. It will have serious consequences for a growing and recent Democracy too. America has a two hundred year history of Independence while Nigeria has only a forty six year old Democracy, which has been off and on at different times because of military interventions. The mass confusion in the American Church and politics, if imported into Nigeria, will crush the young Nation. God forbid!

CHAPTER NINE:

MY BILL OF RIGHTS

Having seen the way life has been twisted in favor of depravity and self indulgence by a big segment of the American population, and feeling some emancipation of my own as part of the product of Freedom, Civil rights and First Amendment Rights, I have come up with my own Bill of Rights too.

Whereas we have assembled on this precious land from all parts of the world to forge our own destiny as a people unlike any other on this planet with emphasis on our freedoms, I declare these rights:

First Right: Congress shall not interfere with any individual or group of individuals doing drugs of any kind in their habitat if such individual or individuals believe that it is good for them to engage in that kind of behavior.

Second Right: Congress or any State in the Federation shall make no laws prescribing what side of the road one should drive on or impose on an American subject any speed limit. (Freedom to choose)

Third right: No Congress or State Government shall make any laws prohibiting a sexual encounter between a minor and an adult, if the two parties agreed to it!

Fourth Right: Since abortion is legal in the United States of America, killing anyone for any reason whatsoever becomes a legal right too, provided the aggressor thinks or feels that he or she has a need to kill, or feels better after killing the person.

Fifth Right: No Congress or State Government has the power to make laws curtailing or limiting anybody's freedom to steal, rape, abuse, or oppress any other individual or limit any other action that the thief, rapist or oppressor feels should be inflicted on the said individual or individuals for that matter.

Sixth Right: Since all American children are the products of the society, which raised them and since, as Americans, they are free to do whatever they like as a First Amendment Right, no Government Federal or State shall put any American in Jail or Prison because it would be cruel and unusual punishment.

Seventh Right: Congress shall make no laws regarding the possession or use of guns by American citizens. Any American citizen could use firearms any where, any time.

Eight Right: Congress shall not recognize any religious practice on the land because religion divides people.

Ninth Right: Since laws are inexhaustible, no Government, Federal or State shall make laws to stop a group of individuals to start or make their own set of laws to suit them, provided the group is made up of men and women of this nation.

Tenth Right: No Government, State or Federal can make laws limiting the number of wives or husbands any American can have and all children are answerable to the State, not the parents.

These laws are absolute and final. Nobody but I can abrogate, change or amend any of these laws, which shall be binding on all Americans.

BIBLIOGRAPHY:

In putting this book together, I made a lot of observations of things around me, watched news bulletins on radio and television and of course, did a lot of research in books and newspapers going back to the late eighties. I am grateful to all the sources I used including but not limited to the following books.

BARTON, David: The Myth of Separation
    Wall-Builder Press
    P.O. Box 397, Aledo, Texas 76008

DAVIS, John Jefferson: Evangelical Ethics
    P &R Publishing P. O. Box 817
    Phillipsburg, N. J. 08865

FALOLA, Toyin: The History of Nigeria
    Greenwood Press, Westport
    Connecticut, (London) 1999

FLINT, John E: Nigeria and Ghana
    Princeton Hall, Inc.
    Englewood Cliffs, N. J.

FOGEL, Daniel: "Africa in Struggle" National Liberation and Proletarian Revolution.
    Ism Press – San Francisco. 2nd Ed. 1986

HARMON, Daniel E.: Exploration of Africa: The Emerging Nations – Nigeria:
    Chelsea House Publishers. Philadelphia

HARTMAN, Gary; MERSKY, Roy M. TATE, Cindy L. :"Landmark Supreme Court Cases".
    Facts on File, Inc., 132 W. 31st St.
    New York, N. Y. 10001

NORRIS, David A.: Lasting Success
Heartland Publications, Inc.
1616 Grand Ave., Ames, Iowa.

SHIVER, Chuck: The Rape of the American Constitution.
Loompanics Unlimited, P. O. Box 1197,
Port Townsend, WA. 98368 (1995)

TUSHNET, Mark: A Court Divided: The Rehnquist Court and
Future of Constitutional Law.
W. W. Norton and Company-New York, London.

ARTICLES

DIONNE, E. J. (Jr.) "Abortion debate turns constructive"
An article: San Francisco Chronicles, May 17, 2005.

GROCHOLEWSKI, Zenon Cardinal Prefect, Congregation for
Catholic Education:

MILLER, Michael J., C.S.B. Titular Arch. Of Vertara, Secretary,
Congregation for Catholic Education: Document on Homosexuals
in the Priesthood.
An article: INSIDE THE VATICAN Magazine. December 2005.

MORSE, Pat: The Real Presence: But, Do I Believe?
An article: INSIDE THE VATICAN Magazine. December, 2005.

RABEL, Andrew:: What will be the Consequences of the Synod?
An article: Interview of Cardinal Francis Arinze, Prefect of the
Congregation for Divine Worship by Andrew Rabel. INSIDE
THE VATICAN Magazine, December, 2005.

ZEHNDER, Christopher: Who Knows How Things Will Change?
"Womanpriest" saying "Mass" at San Jose State:
An article: San Francisco Faith.